Rhetoric, Logic,

Teacher's Edition

& Argumentation:

A Guide for Student Writers

PRESTWICK HOUSE

Proud to Be on the Teacher's Side

Senior Editor:
Paul Moliken

Writer:
Magedah E. Shabo

Reviewing Teachers:
*Shannon Ginn, Bernadine M. Srocki, Michelle Peeling,
Judith Mayersmith, Jodi Gray Kahn, Elizabeth Miley,
Leticia Geldart, Barbara Schnoor, Karen F. Jones, Pauline
Lakanen, Robert Ver Straten, Cynthia Byers*

Cover and Text Design:
Larry Knox

Layout and Production:
Jeremy Clark

PRESTWICK HOUSE
Proud to Be on the Teacher's Side

© 2010 Copyrighted by Prestwick House, Inc.

Printed in the United States of America.

ISBN: 978-1-60843-973-7

Item No. 305056

Rhetoric, Logic, & Argumentation:
A Guide for Student Writers

Table of Contents

Introduction
Rhetoric, Logic, & Argumentation

IN THE MODERN LANGUAGE-ARTS CLASSROOM, students are trained in the basics of grammar, writing, and reading comprehension, but they are often left to fend for themselves when it comes to the more difficult tasks of analysis and persuasion. Students are often required to form and analyze arguments without ever having been taught the basic rules of reasoning, and they're asked to express their arguments in a compelling style without having learned any of the established techniques of rhetorical persuasion.

Taking a cue from the classical approach to education, with its emphasis on rhetoric and logic, *Rhetoric, Logic, and Argumentation* explains some of the essential approaches to communication and reasoning that any student writer should understand. Beginning with an introduction to the three rhetorical appeals (ethical, pathetic, and logical), the book goes on to explain the basics of logic, introducing students to deductive and inductive reasoning, and a variety of common logical fallacies. This guide provides students with the tools they will need to both analyze the arguments they encounter and compose their own persuasive messages. After completing this book and the accompanying exercises, students should find that they have a greater command of the techniques of argumentation and a more purposeful approach to writing.

Reader's Notes: Terms that appear in bold italics on their first occurrence are defined in the glossary at the back of the book. Many of these terms have been used in past AP Language and Composition Examinations.

Rhetoric in Argumentation

*"the art of ruling the
minds of men"*

PLATO

Rhetorical Appeals

THERE ARE MANY DEFINITIONS for the term *rhetoric*, but Plato may have put it best when he described it as "the art of ruling the minds of men." In more literal terms, **rhetoric** can be defined as "the technique or study of communication and persuasion." The study of rhetoric is an immense topic, but this book will cover the basic modes of persuasive communication.

First, there are three main elements to consider in crafting an argument: the **speaker,** the **audience**, and the **message**. All efforts at communication focus on one or more of these elements. In this book, we use the term "speaker" for the individual who is delivering the message, whether in writing, speech, or another medium. The "audience" is the person or group of people who will receive the "message"—the information the speaker attempts to convey to the audience.

> **Etymology:** The English word "rhetoric" is derived from the Greek *rhetor*, which means "orator." It is also closely linked to the term *rhema*, which means "that which is spoken." In its modern usage, "rhetoric" describes any form of persuasive verbal communication, whether oral or written.

speaker: the individual who is delivering the message, whether in writing, speech, or another medium (i.e., the writer, orator, or presenter)

audience: the person or people who receive the message (i.e., the readers, listeners, or observers)

message: the information the speaker wishes to convey to the audience (i.e., the argument, topic, or thesis)

A skilled communicator will keep each of these three components in mind while formulating and presenting an argument. The three elements are often depicted as parts of a triangle, which illustrates their mutually supportive relationship. Just as a triangle has three sides, a well-crafted message will consider each of these three factors.

speaker

audience

message

The Three Rhetorical Appeals

The communication triangle we've just discussed was derived from Aristotle's fourth-century B.C. *Treatise on Rhetoric*, which describes three different modes of persuasion—one focused on the sender of the message, one on the receiver, and one on the message itself. We categorize these classical appeals that Aristotle describes using the Greek words *ethos*, *pathos*, and *logos*.

In Aristotle's words,

> *Of the modes of persuasion furnished by the spoken word there are three kinds. The first kind depends on the **personal character of the speaker** [ethos]; the second on **putting the audience into a certain frame of mind** [pathos]; the third on the proof, or apparent **proof, provided by the words of the speech itself** [logos].*[1]

ethos: moral character. In an *appeal to ethos*, also known as an ethical appeal, the speaker emphasizes the strength of his or her own moral character and experience in order to establish personal credibility.

pathos: emotion. An *appeal to pathos* attempts to elicit an emotional response from the audience.

logos:[2] reason, logic, words. An *appeal to logos* relies on the use of rational analysis and persuasive language.

Ethos (speaker)
Pathos (audience)
Logos (message)

Earlier, we arranged the elements of communication around the three points of a triangle. We can now replace the elements of speaker, audience, and message with their corresponding classical approaches. Ethos is an approach that's focused on the speaker, pathos on the audience, and logos on the message.

Although we describe each of these appeals as a separate mode of persuasion, the most effective communications are those that subtly and seamlessly combine all three of these approaches. Ideally, an argument should establish the speaker's credibility (whether directly or implicitly), engage the emotions of the audience, and be founded in solid logic, eloquently expressed. The following chapters discuss each appeal separately.

---

[1] From Aristotle's *Treatise on Rhetoric*. The words "ethos," "pathos," and "logos" have been added.
[2] The word "logos" has a variety of meanings, but we have limited our definition to fit the context of rhetorical appeals.

Exercise: Identification

Identify the term from the word bank that best matches each description.

> **logos, pathos, rhetoric, audience, ethos, message, speaker**

1. Related to the audience's feelings

2. "The art of ruling the minds of men"

3. Emphasizes reason and proof

4. The individual(s) on the receiving end of the communication

5. The individual presenting the argument in speech, writing, or another medium

6. The ideas being communicated

7. Emphasizes the speaker's character

Appeal to Ethos

An appeal to ethos (ethical appeal) calls attention to positive characteristics of the speaker as a means of adding credibility to an argument. The speaker attempts to appear principled, competent, authoritative, and likable. In creating this image, the speaker gains the audience's favor, increasing the likelihood that the message will be accepted and believed. Forming an ethical appeal is similar to the process of creating a "reliable narrator" when writing fiction—it is the process of developing a trust-worthy and believable persona.

In the following quote from Congressman and presidential candidate Ron Paul, we see a clear and straightforward example of an appeal to ethos.

> *As an O.B. doctor of thirty years, and having delivered 4,000 babies, I can assure you life begins at conception. I am legally responsible for the unborn, no matter what I do, so there's a legal life there. The unborn has inheritance rights, and if there's an injury or a killing, there is a legal entity. There is no doubt about it.*

Here, Paul prefaces his argument against legalized abortion by highlighting his background as an obstetrician who has delivered thousands of babies. By mentioning his thirty years as a medical doctor, Paul establishes his credibility and authority on the topic at hand. Identifying with the medical profession also allows Paul to benefit from the positive stereotypes that label doctors as people of considerable intelligence and character.

The quote from Ron Paul is an example of an overt appeal to ethos, in which the speaker explicitly describes his or her credentials or other positive personal traits to gain an audience's trust. However, many appeals to ethos are made in a subtler manner. For example, in some cases, a speaker will candidly confess some negative trait to appear honest and humble, hoping to gain an audience's trust. Perhaps the subtlest form of ethical appeal is simply using proper grammar and polite conventions of speech or behavior in order to appear well educated, intelligent, and likable.

The appeal to ethos is a tool that all speakers should use; it has considerable persuasive power, and when used properly, it can add useful information to a debate. Ethical appeals must be made with great care, however, because they can sometimes be misleading. In some cases, an ethical appeal can turn into a fallacious **argument from authority**,[3] in which a speaker insists that an argument is true simply because a so-called expert affirms it. This approach is illogical and should be avoided. To determine whether an ethical appeal is being used correctly, ask yourself whether the information that's provided about the speaker is presented honestly, without exaggeration, and whether the information is adequately supported by a logical argument.

The following speech presents an example of an ethos-centered approach to expressing an argument. In this brief address, delivered spontaneously by Sojourner Truth at a women's convention in 1851 and transcribed by an observer, Truth argues that women should be treated as equals with men and uses her own experience and her own character to illustrate her argument. Observe the techniques she uses and the impressions they create.

---

[3] This is a logical fallacy that will be discussed in greater detail later in the book.

"Ain't I a Woman?"

Well, CHILDREN, where there is so much racket there must be something out of kilter. I think that 'twixt the Negroes of the South and the women at the North, all talking about rights, the white men will be in a fix pretty soon. But what's all this here talking about?

> The speech begins with Sojourner Truth addressing the audience as "children." This creates an affable, informal tone and establishes Truth's image as a motherly figure.

That man over there says that women need to be helped into carriages, and lifted over ditches, and to have the best place everywhere. Nobody ever helps me into carriages, or over mud-puddles, or gives me any best place! And ain't I a woman? Look at me! Look at my arm! I have ploughed and planted, and gathered into barns, and no man could head me! And ain't I a woman? I could work as much and eat as much as a man—when I could get it—and bear the lash as well! And ain't I a woman? I have borne thirteen children, and seen most all sold off to slavery, and when I cried out with my mother's grief, none but Jesus heard me! And ain't I a woman?

> In this passage, Truth describes her own experiences to establish her expertise on the subject of how women differ from men. Through the experiences she lists here, Truth demonstrates that she has firsthand knowledge of how hard women can work and the kinds of hardships they are capable of surviving. Truth's testimony of her own strength and perseverance makes her a credible witness on the subject of women's abilities. (Note that this is not an argument from authority because Truth is using herself as an example, rather than using her opinion as the defining point of the argument.)

Then they talk about this thing in the head; what's this they call it? [A member of the audience whispers, "intellect."] That's it, honey. What's that got to do with women's rights or Negroes' rights? If my cup won't hold but a pint, and yours holds a quart, wouldn't you be mean not to let me have my little half measure full?

> Truth makes herself appear humble and likable through self-deprecating humor.

Then that little man in black there, he says women can't have as much rights as men, 'cause Christ wasn't a woman! Where did your Christ come from? Where did your Christ come from? From God and a woman! Man had nothing to do with Him.

> Here, Truth again makes an attempt at humor to establish rapport with the audience.

If the first woman God ever made was strong enough to turn the world upside down all alone, these women together ought to be able to turn it back, and get it right side up again! And now they is asking to do it, the men better let them.

Obliged to you for hearing me, and now old Sojourner ain't got nothing more to say.

> In another display of modesty, Truth thanks the audience for hearing her and refers to herself as "old Sojourner."

Truth's ethical appeals in this argument defy expectations: rather than presenting herself as highly educated and erudite, she embodies a simple, plainspoken persona. In so doing, she comes across as likable, trustworthy, and world-wise. In many cases, downplaying one's personal abilities, as Truth does here, is even more effective than highlighting them.

Ethical appeals can take many forms, and most arguments will be presented with some regard to ethos, even if the speaker never makes any specific reference to him- or herself; even the decision to remain formal and distant can be a part of a speaker's ethos. Every detail of a composition can reflect in some way on the speaker, and must, therefore, be chosen wisely.

Exercise: Analysis

In 399 B.C., Socrates was tried for having corrupted the youth of Athens for defying Greek religious teachings. Before being sentenced to death, Socrates spoke in his own defense at his trial. The following excerpt comes from the beginning of Socrates' address to the jury, as rendered by his student Plato.

Read the following passage carefully. Then, identify and describe Socrates' methods in presenting a persuasive ethos. Be sure to name the specific qualities Socrates attempts to embody, and include examples from the text to illustrate your points.

Note to teachers: Student responses will vary, but may include some of the points that follow in the margin notes.

I KNOW NOT, O Athenians, how you may be affected by my accusers: I indeed have through them almost forgotten myself, so persuasively have they spoken; though, as I may say, they have not asserted anything which is true. But among the multitude of their false assertions I am most surprised at this, in which they say that you ought to beware of being deceived by me, as if I were an eloquent speaker. For that they should not be ashamed of asserting that which will be immediately confuted by me in reality, since in the present instance I shall appear to you to be by no means eloquent, this seems to me to be the consummation of impudence, unless they call him eloquent who speaks the truth. For, if they assert this, I shall indeed acknowledge myself to be a rhetorician, though not according to their conceptions. They have not then, as I said, asserted anything which is true; but from me you will hear all the truth. Not, by Jupiter, O Athenians, that you will hear from me a discourse splendidly decorated with nouns and verbs, and adorned in other respects like the harangues of these men; but you will hear me speaking in such language as may casually present itself. For I am confident that what I say will be just, nor let any one of you expect it will be otherwise: for it does not become one of my age to come before you like a lad with a studied discourse. And, indeed, I very much request and beseech you, O Athenians, that if you should hear me apologizing in the same terms and modes of expression which I am accustomed to use in the Forum, on the Exchange and Public Banks, and in other places, where many of you have heard me, that you will neither wonder nor be disturbed on this account; for the case is as follows: I now for the first time come before this tribunal, though I am more than seventy years old; and consequently I am a stranger to the mode of speaking which is here adopted. As, therefore, if I were

Acknowledging the strength of his accusers' presentation, Socrates comes across as honest and candid.

Socrates explicitly asserts his honesty and his intention to be candid and plainspoken, inviting the audience's trust.

Socrates mentions his advanced age, which is often associated with wisdom, and asserts that he intends to be honorable in his self-defense.

Socrates again mentions his age, this time in a way that invites sympathy. Here, Socrates is pointing out the fact that at over seventy years of age, he is being called to speak in a court setting for the first time.

in reality a foreigner, you would pardon me for using the language and the manner in which I had been educated, so now I request you, and this justly, as it appears to me, to suffer the mode of my diction, whether it be better or worse, and to attend to this, whether I speak what is just or not: for this is the virtue of a judge, as that of an orator is to speak the truth.

Socrates makes a long apology for his manner of speaking, which he suggests might not be suitable for the present occasion. He describes his naiveté on the subject of the court's customs in a way that's meant to make him appear simple and innocent.

Appeal to Pathos

Appeals to pathos, also known as "pathetic" appeals, focus on the audience's feelings, setting an emotional tone through the use of provocative language, imagery, and information. This technique is often used to incite an audience to take a specific course of action, from donating to a charitable cause to initiating a war.

For an example of an appeal to pathos, consider the following excerpt from the "Letter from Birmingham Jail," an open letter written by Martin Luther King, Jr., in 1963. Here, King explains his sense of urgency in actively pursuing an end to racial segregation, responding to the suggestion that the matter should be left for the courts to decide.

> Perhaps it is easy for those who have never felt the stinging darts of segregation to say, 'Wait.' But when you have seen vicious mobs lynch your mothers and fathers at will and drown your sisters and brothers at whim; when you have seen hate-filled policemen curse, kick and even kill your black brothers and sisters; when you see the vast majority of your twenty million Negro brothers smothering in an airtight cage of poverty in the midst of an affluent society; when you suddenly find your tongue twisted and your speech stammering as you seek to explain to your six-year-old daughter why she can't go to the public amusement park that has just been advertised on television, and see tears welling up in her eyes when she is told that Funtown is closed to colored children, and see ominous clouds of inferiority beginning to form in her little mental sky . . . when you are forever fighting a degenerating sense of 'nobodiness'—then you will understand why we find it difficult to wait.

This passage illustrates an honest and effective use of the pathetic appeal as a call to action. In this example, King describes painful situations that he and others are facing as evidence that a great deal of suffering is taking place and that an end to segregation is urgently needed. In the context of the letter, King's emotionally provocative descriptions complement a well-reasoned argument for ending segregation right away.

When used properly, pathetic appeals should do just that—they should add a sense of life and urgency to an argument that is well-founded in reason. Unfortunately, however, the technique is often abused through fallacious emotional appeals,[4] which evoke strong feelings not to supplement logical arguments, but to supersede them.

---

[4] The logical fallacy of emotional appeal is discussed in a later chapter.

To determine if an appeal to pathos is being used honestly and appropriately, take a careful look at what the speaker is attempting to persuade the audience to do. If the speaker hopes to arouse the audience to follow some course of action that is directly related to the emotion in question, the pathetic appeal may be appropriate. By contrast, a fallacious emotional appeal will encourage the audience to come to a given conclusion based on emotions alone, with little or no regard for logic.

Unfortunately, distinguishing between appropriate and inappropriate uses of the pathetic mode of persuasion can be a highly **subjective** process. For an example of a more **ambiguous** use of pathos, we can look to Mark Antony's speech to the Roman crowd in Shakespeare's *Julius Caesar*. In this passage from Act III, scene ii, of the play, Caesar has just been murdered by his closest friend, Brutus, and several other statesmen he had considered friends. Brutus is planning to take over Caesar's position and has just given a speech that was well received by the crowd. In the excerpts that follow, Mark Antony is attempting to arouse disgust and outrage in the Roman people over Caesar's murder, hoping to keep Brutus from rising as Caesar's successor.

ANTONY:
Friends, Romans, countrymen, lend me your ears;
I come to bury Caesar, not to praise him.
The evil that men do lives after them;
The good is oft interred with their bones;
So let it be with Caesar. The noble Brutus
Hath told you Caesar was ambitious:
If it were so, it was a grievous fault,
And grievously hath Caesar answer'd it.
Here, under leave of Brutus and the rest--
For Brutus is an honorable man;
So are they all, all honorable men--
Come I to speak in Caesar's funeral.
He was my friend, faithful and just to me:
But Brutus says he was ambitious;
And Brutus is an honorable man.
He hath brought many captives home to Rome
Whose ransoms did the general coffers fill:
Did this in Caesar seem ambitious?
When that the poor have cried, Caesar hath wept:
Ambition should be made of sterner stuff:
Yet Brutus says he was ambitious;
And Brutus is an honorable man.
You all did see that on the Lupercal
I thrice presented him a kingly crown,
Which he did thrice refuse: was this ambition?
Yet Brutus says he was ambitious;
And, sure, he is an honorable man.
I speak not to disprove what Brutus spoke,
But here I am to speak what I do know.

> Antony addresses his hearers as "friends" and "countrymen" to establish a sense of camaraderie.

> Antony arouses sympathy in the audience by reminding them that Caesar was his personal friend.

> By describing Caesar's military accomplishments, generosity, and compassion for the common people, Antony encourages the crowd to remember Caesar with fondness, pity, and affection.

You all did love him once, not without cause:
What cause withholds you then, to mourn for him?
O judgment! thou art fled to brutish beasts,
And men have lost their reason. Bear with me;
My heart is in the coffin there with Caesar,
And I must pause till it come back to me.
If you have tears, prepare to shed them now.
You all do know this mantle: I remember
The first time ever Caesar put it on;
'Twas on a summer's evening, in his tent,
That day he overcame the Nervii:
Look, in this place ran Cassius' dagger through:
See what a rent the envious Casca made:
Through this the well-beloved Brutus stabb'd;
And as he pluck'd his cursed steel away,
Mark how the blood of Caesar follow'd it,
As rushing out of doors, to be resolved
If Brutus so unkindly knock'd, or no;
For Brutus, as you know, was Caesar's angel:
Judge, O you gods, how dearly Caesar loved him!
This was the most unkindest cut of all;
For when the noble Caesar saw him stab,
Ingratitude, more strong than traitors' arms,
Quite vanquish'd him: then burst his mighty heart;
And, in his mantle muffling up his face,
Even at the base of Pompey's statue,
Which all the while ran blood, great Caesar fell.
O, what a fall was there, my countrymen!
Then I, and you, and all of us fell down,
Whilst bloody treason flourish'd over us.
O, now you weep; and, I perceive, you feel
The dint of pity: these are gracious drops.
Kind souls, what, weep you when you but behold
Our Caesar's vesture wounded? Look you here,
Here is himself, marr'd, as you see, with traitors.

Here, Antony attempts to inspire a sense of guilt in his audience.

In demonstrating his sorrow over Caesar's death, Antony both solicits pity for himself and convinces the crowd that they should join him in mourning.

With nostalgia and sorrow, Antony presents Caesar's coat to the crowd and reminisces on the first time Caesar wore it

Here, Antony incites the crowd's anger by describing the cut marks in the coat and prompting his audience to envision Brutus' violent act.

Next, Antony points out the great love Caesar had for Brutus, inspiring both pity for Caesar and indignation at Brutus' treachery.

Antony encourages the crowd to empathize with the fallen Caesar and take offense on Caesar's behalf.

Antony compliments the crowd's sensitivity before drawing their attention toward Caesar's corpse, encouraging his listeners to become even more emotional.

Through this speech, Antony hopes to convince his audience to distrust Caesar's would-be successors on the grounds that they have murdered an innocent man. By describing the violent act of Caesar's murder with vivid imagery and emotionally charged language, Mark Antony hopes to excite a sense of moral outrage in his fellow citizens and to persuade them not to trust Brutus or place him in a position of power. If this is indeed Antony's only goal in making this speech, it seems an honorable one. Even so, arguments that rely heavily on pathos will always be subject to suspicion. If the speaker relies more heavily on emotion than on logic, as Antony does in this speech, audience members might feel that they are being unfairly manipulated. Ultimately, whether just or unjust, the pathetic approach Antony uses demonstrates both the power and the danger inherent in arousing an audience's emotions.

Exercise: Analysis

In Harper Lee's To Kill a Mockingbird, *attorney Atticus Finch defends a black client who has been charged with raping a white woman in 1930s Alabama. The following passage is an excerpt from Atticus's closing argument before an all-white jury, taken from the film adaptation of the novel. In this speech, Atticus summarizes his claim that the alleged victim of the crime has falsely accused the defendant, Tom Robinson, to cover up her own romantic interest in him.*

Read the following speech carefully. Then, identify and describe Atticus's methods in presenting his appeals to pathos. Be sure to name the specific emotional tones that Finch's words elicit, using examples from the text to illustrate your points.

Note to teachers: Student responses will vary, but may include some of the points that follow in the margin notes.

I HAVE NOTHING BUT PITY in my heart for the chief witness for the State. She is the victim of cruel poverty and ignorance. But my pity does not extend so far as to her putting a man's life at stake, which she has done in an effort to get rid of her own guilt. Now I say "guilt," gentlemen, because it was guilt that motivated her. She's committed no crime. She has merely broken a rigid and time-honored code of our society—a code so severe that whoever breaks it is hounded from our midst as unfit to live with. She must destroy the evidence of her offense. But what was the evidence of her offense? Tom Robinson, a human being. She must put Tom Robinson away from her. Tom Robinson was to her a daily reminder of what she did. Now, what did she do? She tempted a Negro. She was white, and she tempted a Negro. She did something that, in our society, is unspeakable. She kissed a black man . . . .

And so, a quiet, humble, respectable Negro, who has had the unmitigated temerity to feel sorry for a white woman, has had to put his word against two white people's. The defendant is not guilty, but somebody in this courtroom is. Now, gentlemen, in this country, our courts are the great levelers. In our courts, all men are created equal. I'm no idealist to believe firmly in the integrity of our courts and of our jury system. That's no ideal to me. That is a living, working reality! Now I am confident that you gentlemen will review without passion the evidence that you have heard, come to a decision and restore this man to his family. In the name of God, do your duty. In the name of God, believe Tom Robinson.

Initially, Atticus portrays Mayella Ewell as a victim, deserving of his and the jury's pity. Realizing that the jury will probably be inclined to take her side, he attempts to evoke sympathy toward her, rather than anger.

By using the emotionally charged phrase "putting a man's life at stake," Atticus expresses the dire importance of the situation at hand.

In an effort to awaken a sense of moral outrage in the jurors, Atticus suggests that Mayella is attempting to destroy and dispose of a human being.

By describing Tom in these positive terms and pointing out his disadvantaged position in the trial, Atticus invites the audience's sympathy.

Atticus demonstrates enthusiasm for the ideals of justice and morality, hoping to inspire the jurors.

He ends the argument with a desperate plea to the jurors, appealing to both their sympathy and their sense of honor.

Appeal to Logos

The appeal to logos (logical appeal) is the most important of the three classical approaches to persuasion, and, as such, it will be the main focus of the remainder of this book. While each of the three modes of communication can be valuable, the logical mode is the most essential—it is the base upon which the other appeals must rest.

While ethos requires the audience to intuit a speaker's true intentions and pathos appeals to an audience's subjective feelings, logos appeals to the rational mind. It is the most **objective** of the three modes, focusing on proof and reason, rather than on perceptions and emotions. In most situations, a speaker should emphasize logos when crafting a message, using ethos and pathos to supplement the argument's logical foundation by adding credibility and emotional force to the message.

Most arguments appeal to a combination of the three modes of thought, so it can be difficult to isolate examples of arguments that are purely logical. There are, however, some instances in which self-referential appeals to ethos and the emotionally charged language of pathos are kept to a minimum. The following argument, an excerpt from Martin Luther's "Ninety-Five Theses,"[5] is an example of an argument that's as close to pure logos as possible.

1. *Our Lord and Master Jesus Christ, when He said 'Poenitentiam agite,'[6] willed that the whole life of believers should be repentance.*
2. *This word cannot be understood to mean sacramental penance, i.e., confession and satisfaction, which is administered by the priests.*
3. *Yet it means not inward repentance only; nay, there is no inward repentance which does not outwardly work diverse mortifications of the flesh.*
4. *The penalty [of sin], therefore, continues so long as hatred of self continues; for this is the true inward repentance, and continues until our entrance into the kingdom of heaven.*

In this example, Luther presents his argument with as little reference to himself and with as little emotion as possible. The result is a message that is somewhat passive and impersonal. But, while that might not sound like a positive description, this "just the facts" tone is actually well suited to this situation; Luther knew that his "Ninety-Five Theses," which protested several of the Roman Catholic Church's practices, raised a controversial subject. By removing himself from the message as much as possible and using an unemotional approach, Luther makes his controversial argument sound unbiased and objective.

The same principle motivates students and scholars to use the passive voice in scholarly writing. Likewise, a judge might state his or her personal decision using the phrase "it is the opinion of the court," rather than the more personal "I think." In situations that call for a high level of objectivity and formality, a speaker will use an impersonal tone and keep ethical and emotional appeals to a minimum.

---

[5] The full title of Luther's work is "Ninety-Five Theses on the Power and Efficacy of Indulgences." Luther nailed this message to the door of the Castle Church in Wittenberg, Germany, in 1517.
[6] Latin for "repent, ye."

In most situations, however, it is appropriate and helpful to incorporate some degree of ethical or pathetic appeal into an argument based on logos. To illustrate what this might look like, let's consider the following passage, also composed by Luther.

MOST SERENE EMPEROR, and your illustrious princes and gracious lords:—I this day appear before you in all humility, according to your command, and I implore your majesty and your august highnesses, by the mercies of God, to listen with favor to the defense of a cause which I am well assured is just and right. I ask pardon, if by reason of my ignorance, I am wanting in the manners that befit a court; for I have not been brought up in king's palaces, but in the seclusion of a cloister. Two questions were yesterday put to me by his imperial majesty; the first, whether I was the author of the books whose titles were read; the second, whether I wished to revoke or defend the doctrine I have taught. I answered the first, and I adhere to that answer.

As to the second, I have composed writings on very different subjects. In some I have discussed Faith and Good Works, in a spirit at once so pure, clear, and Christian, that even my adversaries themselves, far from finding anything to censure, confess that these writings are profitable, and deserve to be perused by devout persons. The pope's bull, violent as it is, acknowledges this. What, then, should I be doing if I were now to retract these writings? Wretched man! I alone, of all men living, should be abandoning truths approved by the unanimous voice of friends and enemies, and opposing doctrines that the whole world glories in confessing! I have composed, secondly, certain works against popery, wherein I have attacked such as by false doctrines, irregular lives, and scandalous examples, afflict the Christian world, and ruin the bodies and souls of men. And is not this confirmed by the grief of all who fear God? Is it not manifest that the laws and human doctrines of the popes entangle, vex, and distress the consciences of the faithful, while the crying and endless extortions of Rome engulf the property and wealth of Christendom, and more particularly of this illustrious nation? If I were to revoke what I have written on that subject, what should I do… but strengthen this tyranny, and open a wider door to so many and flagrant impieties? Bearing down all resistance with fresh fury, we should behold these proud men swell, foam, and rage more than ever! And not merely would the yoke which now weighs down Christians be made more grinding by my retraction—it would thereby become, so to speak, lawful,—for, by my retraction, it would receive confirmation from your most serene majesty, and all the States of the Empire.

By addressing his audience in highly complimentary terms and requesting mercy, Luther appeals to his audience's feelings of pity and pride (pathos).

By apologizing for his unsophisticated manners, Luther demonstrates humility (ethos).

Luther begins to explain why he cannot denounce all of his books by pointing out that some of them have been widely praised, even by his adversaries. He explains that logically, by denying everything he has said before, he would be contradicting some of the most basic beliefs that he and his accusers share.

Here, Luther goes on to explain why he cannot retract his more controversial works that criticize the Roman Catholic Church—he believes that his accusations are true and that if he denied what he had previously stated on the matter, he would be complicit in the Church's crimes. Luther uses emotional language to describe the suffering of the common people under the Roman doctrines, which he says "entangle, vex, and distress" people of faith. These words reflect Luther's motivation for publishing his works: he is frustrated by what he sees as the mistreatment of others.

.... I cannot submit my faith either to the pope or to the council, because it is as clear as noonday that they have fallen into error and even into glaring inconsistency with themselves. If, then, I am not convinced by proof from Holy Scripture, or by cogent reasons, if I am not satisfied by the very text I have cited, and if my judgment is not in this way brought into subjection to God's word, I neither can nor will retract anything; for it cannot be right for a Christian to speak against his conscience. I stand here and can say no more. God help me. Amen.

Luther concludes by explaining that he will recant his works only if someone can persuade him through logic and proof (from scripture) that his previous statements have been wrong.

These passages are excerpts from a speech Luther presented before a Roman Catholic assembly when he was called to recant his controversial works. Luther's speech is founded in reason and emphasizes the importance of proof. At the same time, however, it also contains subtle ethical and pathetic appeals; it is not strictly facts and reasons, like the "Ninety-Five Theses." Since Luther is, in this case, defending his own thoughts and motivations, it is fitting that he should take care to present some evidence of his personal character and some indication of his feelings.

Keep in mind that not all forms of expression must contain appeals to logos; it is only persuasive rhetoric that must be based on logic. Before evaluating a work on the basis of its logical appeal, or lack thereof, remember to ask what **thesis**, if any, the speaker is attempting to impress upon the audience.

Exercise: Analysis

In 1873, Susan B. Anthony, a leader of the women's suffrage movement, was tried for the crime of voting in a presidential election at a time when voting was illegal for women. The following passage is Anthony's defense against this charge.

Read the passage carefully. Then, describe Anthony's logical argument. Identify specific examples of logical appeals.

Note to teachers: Student responses will vary, but may include some of the points that follow in the margin notes.

FRIENDS AND FELLOW CITIZENS: I stand before you tonight under indictment for the alleged crime of having voted at the last presidential election, without having a lawful right to vote. It shall be my work this evening to prove to you that in thus voting, I not only committed no crime, but, instead, simply exercised my citizen's rights, guaranteed to me and all United States citizens by the National Constitution, beyond the power of any state to deny.

Anthony states her purpose clearly and directly.

The preamble of the Federal Constitution says:

"We, the people of the United States, in order to form a more perfect union, establish justice, ensure domestic tranquility, provide for the common defense, promote the general welfare, and secure the blessings of liberty to ourselves and our posterity, do ordain and establish this Constitution for the United States of America."

This quote from the Preamble to the US Constitution is the foundation upon which Anthony will build her argument.

It was we, the people; not we, the white male citizens; nor yet we, the male citizens; but we, the whole people, who formed the Union. And we formed it, not to give the blessings of liberty, but to secure them; not to the half of ourselves and the half of our posterity, but to the whole people—women as well as men. And it is a downright mockery to talk to women of their enjoyment of the blessings of liberty while they are denied the use of the only means of securing them provided by this democratic-republican government—the ballot.

Anthony uses the wording of the Preamble ("we the people") as the basis for her argument that all people, regardless of sex, should be allowed to vote.

For any state to make sex a qualification that must ever result in the disfranchisement of one entire half of the people, is to pass a bill of attainder, or, an ex post facto law, and is therefore a violation of the supreme law of the land. By it the blessings of liberty are forever withheld from women and their female posterity.

Again appealing to the ideas expressed in the Preamble, Anthony suggests that it is impossible to say that women enjoy "liberty" while they are not allowed to vote.

To them this government has no just powers derived from the consent of the governed. To them this government is not a democracy. It is not a republic. It is an odious aristocracy; a hateful oligarchy of sex; the most hateful aristocracy ever established on the face of the globe; an oligarchy of wealth, where the rich govern the poor. An oligarchy of learning, where the educated govern the ignorant, or even an oligarchy of race, where the Saxon rules the African, might be endured; but this oligarchy of sex, which makes father, brothers, husband, sons, the oligarchs over the mother and sisters, the wife and daughters, of every household—which ordains all men sovereigns, all women subjects, carries dissension, discord, and rebellion into every home of the nation.

In this paragraph, Anthony introduces a bit of emotion to her argument, using anger-inducing words like "hateful" and "odious," and describing unjust situations. However, she ultimately arrives at the idea that an "oligarchy of sex" should not be allowed to exist because it will be inefficient, leading to chaos and disharmony in homes across the country.

Webster, Worcester, and Bouvier all define a citizen to be a person in the United States, entitled to vote and hold office.

The only question left to be settled now is: Are women persons? And I hardly believe any of our opponents will have the hardihood to say they are not. Being persons, then, women are citizens; and no state has a right to make any law, or to enforce any old law, that shall abridge their privileges or immunities. Hence, every discrimination against women in the constitutions and laws of the several states is today null and void, precisely as is every one against Negroes.

Anthony closes with an investigation of the word "persons," and the conclusion, based on the definitions of "Webster, Worcester, and Bouvier," that women and blacks are indeed persons and, therefore, deserve all the rights of personhood.

Logic in Argumentation

"Most people are unable to write because they are unable to think."

H. L. MENCKEN

Why Logic Is Essential to Writing

A S HUMANS, WE ARE BORN with the potential to think rationally. We have a remarkable capacity for inferring meaning and drawing conclusions. Unfortunately, despite its incredible potential for rational thought, the human mind is naturally predisposed to certain kinds of errors. As we will discuss further in the next chapter, all human beings are innately biased in favor of specific kinds of illogical thought patterns.

That's why it's important that we use caution when we express our own ideas or consider the ideas of others; we must guard against passively receiving or carelessly expressing thoughts without first subjecting them to some level of rational scrutiny. It's important that we read and write with an awareness of our mental weaknesses and the weaknesses of others to avoid being persuaded by illogical arguments or making them ourselves.

Fortunately for us, there are systematic methods for studying and assessing the various categories and components of thought and expression to combat the innate shortcomings of the human mind. We have developed a unique language—the language of logic—that enables us to identify and describe the different kinds of thought we use, the components of arguments, and the types of errors in reasoning that people often commit.

The remaining chapters of this book explain some of the fundamental principles of rational thought and argumentation to equip you for the tasks of reading critically and writing rational, well-thought-out arguments. In the following chapters, you will learn to recognize deductive and inductive argument forms, while gaining experience in recognizing and responding to some of the most common kinds of errors in reasoning. This practice should enable you to assess information in a logical manner, form solid, well-thought-out arguments, and dismantle the many faulty arguments you may encounter, whether in the academic world or in real life.

But first, it's important to understand the enemy that lies within: cognitive biases. In the following chapter, we'll explore some of the ways our minds can deceive us.

The Problem: Cognitive Bias

I think, therefore I err.

The human mind is a powerful instrument, with a unique potential for rational thought. But as impressive as our minds may be in their ability to process complex information, they are prone to make mistakes. In fact, scientists have observed that humans are universally inclined to make certain kinds of significant miscalculations. We refer to these tendencies as ***cognitive biases*** because they seem to express a hard-wired preference for certain flawed thought patterns.

When we rely on instinct alone, our cognitive biases often lead us to form incorrect conclusions. Fortunately, as English writer Benjamin Haydon once said, "A bias recognized is a bias sterilized." That is, we can neutralize the effects of our innate biases by learning to recognize and guard against them. Once familiar with the ways in which our minds tend to deceive us, we are more likely to question our instinctive responses and faulty assumptions, and we are better able to see the importance of taking a systematic approach to reasoning.

The following well-known cognitive biases help illustrate some of the ways our minds deceive us and demonstrate the importance of logical thinking:

Confirmation Bias

Confirmation bias is the tendency to view information in a way that validates our existing opinions and beliefs. In other words, we are generally predisposed to be less skeptical of information that corroborates our preconceived ideas than we are of information that contradicts our opinions. We are also more likely to seek and to remember facts and arguments that support our own views. In essence, we search for and cling to information that confirms our already-held beliefs, and we tend to disregard contrary information.

Example: Ignoring any news report or opinion broadcasted by XYZ News because you usually disagree with the channel's commentaries.

Bandwagon Effect

Known by various names, including "herd mentality" and "groupthink," the ***bandwagon effect*** describes the human tendency to make decisions on the basis of the majority opinion. In this phenomenon, people are inclined to view the popularity of a certain point of view as sufficient evidence for the truth of that view, rather than logically evaluating the facts.

Example: Assuming that Che Guevara was an admirable person, without first studying his historical legacy, because your friends wear T-shirts that bear his image.

Wishful Thinking

The term ***wishful thinking*** refers to irrational optimism. An individual who experiences this cognitive bias will form conclusions based on idealized imagined outcomes, rather than by objectively examining the evidence at hand. Because of our bias toward wishful thinking, we tend to predict positive results more often than negative results, even when the positive outcomes we predict defy logic. This fallacy is often described through the cliché of "seeing the world through rose-colored glasses."

Example: Feeling certain that you will win the lottery, despite the fact that your chance of winning is less than one in a million.

Framing Bias

When the same information is presented in different ways, we tend to respond differently based on how the issue is presented, or "framed." This *framing bias* often becomes apparent when an individual is presented with two identical options that are described in different terms.

Example: Preferring a glass that's described as "half full" to one that is "half empty," or thinking that a gallon of ice cream sounds more appealing than four quarts.[7]

Clustering Illusion

When data occur in clusters, people often read meaning into this clustering even if it is completely random. The term *clustering illusion* describes this human tendency to perceive patterns where no pattern exists. This bias is one example of the many ways in which the human mind is inclined to misread statistical data.

Example: Assuming that there is a relationship between weather patterns and days of the week because it has rained every Saturday for the past month.

Gambler's Fallacy

People tend to believe that the results of a random event, like a coin toss, will affect the probability of future outcomes. This mistake in reasoning is known as the *gambler's fallacy*. In reality, the results of a random event will have no effect on future random events; for example, the results of one coin toss will have no effect on the outcome of the next coin toss.

Example: The idea that lightning never strikes the same place twice is based on the gambler's fallacy.

Halo Effect

When we are exposed to a person who has one positive quality, we are more likely to attribute other desirable traits to the individual. Physical attractiveness, for example, can make a person seem more intelligent or honest than he or she really is. This is known as the *halo effect*. The positive trait acts a halo, deflecting blame and inviting positive assumptions.

Example: Voting for the more attractive candidate because "he just seems more honest" than his opponent.

---

[7] Note that the quantities described are equivalent.

Illusory Superiority

The term *illusory superiority* describes the tendency to view oneself as superior to others. Because of this bias, also known as the "better-than-average effect," individuals tend to rate themselves as being above average in positive traits and below average in negative traits.

Example: Believing that you are actually a much safer driver than most, despite your numerous accidents and speeding tickets.

Self-Serving Bias

The *self-serving bias* occurs when an individual claims an undue amount of credit for a positive situation or an inadequate amount of blame for a negative condition.

Example: Taking credit for your daughter's good grades, while blaming her poor study habits on her teacher.

Conclusion: Don't believe everything you think.

The cognitive biases discussed in this chapter are just a few of the many errors that humans are inclined to make. However, even from this small sample, it's easy to see that in many situations, the human mind is set up to fail at properly evaluating information.

We are inclined to see the world in a way that preserves an overly positive self-image and an excessively rosy outlook on the future. Meanwhile, we often view other people in a more negative light and blame them for our own failings. We see patterns where there are none, and we generally tend to misinterpret statistics. Perhaps most significantly, we are naturally wired to block out information and arguments that defy our own beliefs. This final error, confirmation bias, is perhaps the most dangerous of all because it can prevent us from ever learning of the errors in our thinking. In order to reason properly, it's essential that we train ourselves to evaluate information objectively, regardless of our previously held assumptions, by listening impartially to information that might seem to conflict with our views.

Now that we've seen some of the mistakes our minds are inclined to make, we are ready to talk about how we can use logic to evaluate our thinking and to keep our biases in check. In the chapters that follow, we'll discuss the methods of classifying arguments, and we'll learn to recognize some of the most common logical fallacies.

Exercise: Identification

For each of the following statements, identify the type of cognitive bias that is being illustrated. There is only one correct answer for each example.

> **Gambler's Fallacy, Confirmation Bias, Illusory Superiority,
> Bandwagon Effect, Halo Effect, Wishful Thinking,
> Framing Bias, Clustering Illusion, Self-Serving Bias**

1. I've found at least thirty articles that confirm my idea that some people have extrasensory perception. I've also seen reports that disagree, but I haven't read any of them.

2. I don't think anyone actually has ESP; everyone I know says that the whole concept is a myth.

3. I think some people do have psychic abilities; I would love to think that it's possible to predict the future.

4. Some people can foresee the future, but I don't think that people can have psychic abilities.

5. I've noticed that every time I think about my best friend, Jessica, she calls me. That's why I think Jessica has ESP.

6. When I called the psychic hotline, they told me I would be struck by lightning. That just proves that they're not really psychic—I've already been struck by lightning once, so it can't happen again.

7. It wasn't my fault that I ran over my neighbor's cat. The psychic told me it would happen. Being run over was just his destiny.

8. My fortuneteller has such an honest face. I can't help but believe her.

9. Most people believe in silly things like ESP and psychics. Fortunately, I'm smarter than most people.

The Solution: Reasoning and Logic

In the previous chapter, we discussed some of the glitches that are built into the human intellect, and we saw examples of some of the specific situations in which our minds can deceive us. Understanding ourselves and how our own minds operate is an essential part of learning to avoid errors.

The next step is to train ourselves to think clearly—to use reason instead of relying on instinct alone.

Reasoning is the process of gathering meaning and drawing conclusions. It's a unique function of the human mind, distinct from emotion, intuition, sense perception, memory, and superstition. When we reason, we attempt to think objectively; we make an effort to detach from the biases of our individual, subjective experiences in order to arrive at objective truths.

Logic is the formal study of reasoning.[8] It allows us to explain and evaluate our thought processes. English philosopher John Locke once described logic as "the anatomy of thought" because just as an anatomist identifies and studies the parts of a body, a student of logic identifies and studies the elements of thoughts and arguments. Logic gives us a language and a set of rules for evaluating our attempts at reasoning. Having a systematized way of speaking about reasoning also allows us to identify and correct erroneous patterns of thought and to teach the best methods of reasoning to others.

Several of the terms we'll use in this book have unique meanings in the field of logic. One such term is "argument." In logic, an *argument* is a set of connected statements that are meant to prove a particular conclusion.

Example:
1. Broccoli is a vegetable.
2. All vegetables are delicious.
3. Therefore, broccoli is delicious.

Although we don't often see arguments presented in this kind of formal, numbered sequence in real life, we often arrange arguments to fit this pattern when we want to evaluate them from a logical perspective.

Arguments can be found in TV news commentaries, newspaper editorials, textbooks, creative works, commercial advertisements, political speeches, debates, lectures, casual conversations, and in any other forum where ideas are exchanged. Arguments are also an essential part of scholarly writing, from high school term papers to doctoral theses.

The arguments we encounter may sometimes be confused with other forms of communication, like statements of opinion or assertions of fact. Arguments can be identified by their purpose of proving a point through a reasoning process. An argument will consist of at least one premise and one conclusion.

---

[8] The terms "reason" and "logic" are often used synonymously. In this book, however, we'll be using the word "logic" to describe the formal study of reasoning.

A *premise* is a declarative statement that is used to support or prove the point of the argument. The argument's *conclusion* is the idea that the premises are designed to prove; in other words, it is the argument's thesis. In an argument, a conclusion will often include the word "therefore." For an illustration of these concepts, let's look at the premises and conclusion from the previous argument.

Example:

1. Broccoli is a vegetable.	**premise**
2. All vegetables are delicious.	**premise**
3. Therefore, broccoli is delicious.	**conclusion**

There's also a name for the process that links the premises to the conclusion in the preceding argument; in logic, we call this process of making a logical assumption based on the available information *inference*. A single argument can contain multiple inferences, as in the following example, which contains two.

Example:

1. I like foods that are delicious.	**premise**
2. All vegetables are delicious.	**premise**
3. I like all vegetables.	**premise (inferred)**
4. Broccoli is a vegetable.	**premise**
5. Therefore, I like broccoli.	**conclusion (inferred)**

In this example, both the third premise and the conclusion of the argument are inferred; the speaker arrived at each of the two statements by piecing together the information from the preceding premises.

Deductive vs. Inductive Arguments

OUR PATTERNS OF THOUGHT can be broken down into two main categories:[9] ***deductive and inductive reasoning***.

We'll talk about each category in greater detail in the following chapters. But first, let's briefly look at the basic definition of each kind of reasoning and see what distinguishes them from one another.

Deductive Reasoning

In deductive reasoning, we begin by proposing a set of principles. We then form conclusions by making logical inferences from these principles. The conclusion of a properly formed deductive argument is a logical consequence of the premises—it *must* be true if the premises are true. The conclusion will not add any new information to the argument; instead, it will simply combine the principles stated in the premises.

Example:
1. All teachers assign homework.
2. Mrs. O'Neil is a teacher.
3. Therefore, Mrs. O'Neil assigns homework.

As this example illustrates, valid deductive arguments are designed in such a way that if the premises are true, the conclusion must also be true by definition.

One common method of recognizing deductive arguments is to look for conclusions that are more specific than the premises—in other words, an argument that progresses from the general to the specific.

General → Specific

The conclusion of a deductive argument is more specific than the premises in the sense that it is limited in scope by the information the premises provide.

---

[9] A third category of thought, ***abductive reasoning***, is a precursor to deductive and inductive thought. Abductive reasoning is the process of developing a hypothesis or a "hunch" based on a limited amount of information. The hypotheses that result from abductive thinking can be tested only through deductive or inductive reasoning; for that reason, abduction is not discussed in this book.

The conclusion will not add any new information to the argument.

Example:
1. All teachers assign homework.
2. Mrs. O'Neil is a teacher.
3. Therefore, Mrs. O'Neil assigns homework.

This argument illustrates the limited nature of a deductive argument's conclusion. The conclusion that "Mrs. O'Neil assigns homework" simply combines the ideas that "all teachers assign homework" and "Mrs. O'Neil is a teacher." It does not discuss anything that has not already been stated in the premises.

Deductive arguments sometimes have conclusions that seem rather broad, in and of themselves. The next example demonstrates what such an argument might look like.

Example:
1. All mammals are warm-blooded.
2. Whales are mammals.
3. Therefore, all whales are warm-blooded.

In this argument, the conclusion makes a statement about "all whales." Even so, the idea of moving from general to specific still applies. We can still say that the conclusion is more specific than the premises because it merely combines the information provided and does not introduce any new ideas.

As each example demonstrates, "general" and "specific" are relative terms, and they describe the relationship between an argument's premises and conclusion—not the individual components.

To summarize, these are the identifying traits of a deductive argument:

1. The argument aims to prove that the conclusion must be true, by definition, if the premises are true.

2. The conclusion synthesizes the information provided in the premises, but does not add any new information. (In a sense, it is "more specific" than the premises.)

Although we use deductive reasoning all the time, we don't often see deductive arguments explicitly spelled out in everyday life. Deductive arguments are usually presented most explicitly in formal debates or academic settings, particularly in subjects like philosophy and mathematics.

Examples of explicit deductive reasoning:

Mathematics
    If $a = b$ and $c = d$, then $a + c = b + d$.
    $A = b$ and $c = d$.
    Therefore, $a + c = b + d$.

Philosophy
    If I am able to think, then I must exist.
    I think.
    Therefore, I exist.

Inductive Reasoning

Inductive arguments are fundamentally different in purpose from deductive arguments—unlike deductive arguments, they do not intend to prove definitively that a certain conclusion *must* be true. Rather, inductive arguments attempt to prove that a given conclusion is *probably* true.

Example:
    1. All the students I know hate doing homework.
    2. Cynthia is a student.
    3. Therefore, Cynthia probably hates doing homework.

As this example illustrates, inductive arguments are usually built upon specific observations. (This argument is built on the observations that many students hate doing homework and Cynthia is a student.) From these observations, the argument postulates that a given conclusion is *probably* true—although the word "probably" is not always used. (In this example, the conclusion suggests that Cynthia probably hates doing homework.)

In contrast with deductive reasoning, which usually argues from general to specific, *inductive* reasoning is said to progress from specific to general.

Specific → General

In other words, inductive arguments form conclusions that reach beyond the scope of the information provided in the premises. The conclusion of an inductive argument will speculate about possibilities outside of the facts that the premises establish.

The following inductive argument illustrates what is meant by the "specific to general" rule.

Example:
1. Cats often scratch their owners.
2. Janice has several cats.
3. Janice has probably been scratched by a cat.

The conclusion of this argument is an informed guess. Unlike the conclusion of a deductive argument, it is not a necessary logical consequence of the information stated in the premises.

The "specific to general" guideline for inductive arguments can be confusing if taken at face value. If the conclusion of an inductive argument makes a detailed prediction about a single individual, for instance, the conclusion could appear to be "specific." Consider the following example:

Example:
1. Most American citizens speak English.
2. Sarah is an American citizen.
3. Therefore, Sarah probably speaks English.

Although the conclusion of this argument makes a prediction about a single individual, it increases the breadth of the argument in the sense that it adds new information. The argument uses specific observations to form a guess about a given member of that population. The speculative nature of the conclusion and the fact that it proposes a new possibility make it clear that this argument is inductive.

Because of the potential for confusion in the "specific to general" rule, the best way to identify an inductive argument is to look for the following characteristics:

1. The premises attempt to prove that the conclusion is probably true.

2. The conclusion postulates an idea that is not contained in the premises. In a sense, it is further-reaching than the premises and adds new information. (It can be described as progressing from "specific" premises to a relatively "general" conclusion.)

While explicit deductive arguments are usually found in the academic world, inductive arguments are often spelled out in less formal settings. For a real-life example of an inductive argument, consider the following headline, which might resemble headlines you have seen in the news.

Scientists Find Link between Overeating and Obesity

As you read the article, you discover that the scientists are thinking inductively. The article begins with the following claims:

Scientists find a higher incidence of obesity in laboratory rats that were force-fed large quantities of corn than in those that were fed smaller quantities. These findings contribute to a growing body of research that suggests that overeating contributes to obesity in rats, and possibly in other mammals.

In this example of inductive reasoning, the reporter begins with an observation of a specific event: scientists force-fed a particular group of rats large quantities of corn, and the rats became obese. Meanwhile, a similar group of rats that was fed less corn did not become obese. Based on this event, the researchers propose a broad principle: eating large quantities of food promotes obesity.

To get a better understanding of the structure of inductive arguments, let's rewrite this argument in a simpler form.

1. A test group of lab rats was force-fed a large quantity of food, while a control group was fed less.

2. The test group had a higher incidence of obesity than the control group.

3. The high-calorie diets of the test group probably caused the rats to become obese.

As this example demonstrates, inductive arguments are founded upon specific evidence—in this case, the lab experiment. From there, the inductive argument will often build up to a general principle—in this example, the proposition that overeating causes obesity.

Common uses of inductive reasoning include

Political debates
"Where Communism has been tried, it has failed; therefore, Communism is an unsustainable model of government."

Scientific studies
Studies show that smoking cigarettes may cause cancer.

Deductive vs. Inductive

To review, some of the major characteristics that set inductive and deductive arguments apart from one another can be found in the following chart.

Deductive:

Example:

1. All feathered animals are birds.

2. Chicken Little has feathers.

3. Therefore, Chicken Little is a bird.

   - "General → Specific" (Conclusions are limited in scope by the premises.)

   - Conclusions *must* be true if the premises are true.

   - Usually implicit in everyday situations; explicitly spelled out only in academic settings

Inductive:

Example:

1. Chicken Little is a bird.

2. Most birds eat insects.

3. Therefore, Chicken Little probably eats insects.

   - "Specific → General" (Conclusions expand the scope of the argument.)

   - Conclusions are speculative, proposing new ideas that are *probably* true.

   - Often explicitly stated in everyday use, as well as in academic settings

Exercise: Identification

For each of the following scenarios, identify whether the reasoning process employed is deductive or inductive, and explain your answer.

1. A history professor forms a theory about why most of the world's great civilizations have appeared near large bodies of water.

2. A lawyer argues that her client is a kind person who would never commit murder.

3. An editor justifies his placement of a comma, using a popular style guide.

4. A scientist explains why lemons appear yellow to the human eye.

5. A doctor suggests that his patient might have pneumonia, based on her symptoms.

6. A math teacher explains how the rules of geometry apply to a particular word problem.

7. A father explains to his nine-year-old daughter that according to the law, she must go to school.

Analyzing Deductive Arguments

Deduction in Real Life

In your daily life, you probably don't come across many deductive arguments that are stated explicitly, in numbered lists, like most of the examples in this book. However, you probably do encounter deductive reasoning quite often, even if you don't recognize it as such. That's partly because in ordinary speech, people usually don't spell out their arguments as clearly as they do when studying reasoning and logic.

To illustrate what deductive arguments usually look like in real life, we'll translate an explicit, formal argument into more casual language.

Example:
1. Apples are a kind of fruit.
2. All fruits are nutritious.
3. Therefore, apples are nutritious.

Ordinary Speech:
"Apples are a kind of fruit, so they must be nutritious."

In the casual version of this argument there is an unspoken premise. The speaker is suggesting that since apples are a kind of fruit, they must be nutritious. The missing premise here is that all fruit is nutritious.

Here's another example of what deductive arguments look like in common phrasing.

Example:
1. Some senators are lawyers.
2. All senators are at least 30 years old.
3. Therefore, all of the lawyers in the Senate are at least 30 years old.

Ordinary Speech:
"All the lawyers in the Senate are at least 30 years old; that's the age requirement for serving in the Senate."

Each of the deductive arguments we've looked at so far can be categorized as a **syllogism**: a deductive argument composed of two premises (major and minor) and a conclusion.

One of the most famous syllogisms is a simple argument about Socrates; remembering this example will make it easier to identify or construct other syllogisms.

Major Premise:	1. All men are mortal.
Minor Premise:	2. Socrates is a man.
Conclusion:	3. Therefore, Socrates is mortal.

The minor premise of a syllogism always provides the subject of the conclusion (in this example, "Socrates"), while the major premise provides the other part of the statement—the predicate (in this case, the phrase "is mortal"):

Evaluating Deductive Reasoning

One of the main benefits of having a formal system of logic is that it allows us to evaluate an argument objectively. Whether we're scrutinizing our own thoughts or the arguments of others, it's important that we have a set of criteria by which we can assess various reasoning processes. By evaluating an argument through the rules of logic, we can objectively determine its quality and decide whether to accept or reject the ideas it proposes.

In the case of a deductive argument, we begin by evaluating the argument's form.[10] In order to be worthy of consideration, a deductive argument must first be found to have a **valid** form. If the argument is valid, we can then assess whether it is **sound**. The following section will explore the ideas of validity and soundness in logic.

Validity

In casual speech, we often use words like "valid" and "sound" to describe statements or arguments that seem effective or convincing. In logic, however, each of these terms has a distinct meaning, separate from its more familiar usage. The formal concepts of validity and soundness are essential elements in the study of argumentation and reasoning, so let's take a minute to discuss what these terms mean in logic.

Most people use the word "valid" simply to indicate agreement. We might say that someone has raised a valid point if we believe that he or she has made a statement that seems relevant to the topic at hand. Likewise, we might say that an entire argument is valid if it seems rational on an intuitive level. However, while this usage is perfectly appropriate in casual conversation, the word has a different meaning altogether in **formal logic**—and it's important to demonstrate an understanding of the technical meaning of the term "validity" not only for the sake of presenting a strong ethos, but also because it's impossible to fully understand the difference between proper and improper inference without an understanding of this fundamental concept.

In logic, validity means something very specific about an argument's form. A valid argument is one whose premises necessitate its conclusion. This means that in a valid argument, it's impossible to affirm each of the argument's premises and deny the conclusion without contradicting yourself.

---

[10] When we study deductive logic, we're mostly concerned with the form, or structure, of the argument. This emphasis on form is the source of the terms "formal logic," which refers to deductive logic, and "formal fallacies," which are errors in deductive logic.

The following is a famous syllogism that we've used previously in this chapter. Here, we are using this argument as an example of valid deductive reasoning.

1. All men are mortal.
2. Socrates is a man.
3. Therefore, Socrates is mortal.

As you can see, if the premises in this argument are assumed to be true, the conclusion must also be true. It's impossible to make the assertion that both premises are true but the conclusion is false without creating a contradiction. This means that the argument passes the validity test.

1. All men are mortal.	If this is true,
2. Socrates is a man.	and this is true,
3. Therefore, Socrates is mortal.	then this cannot be false.

Validity Test: If it is impossible for the conclusion to be false while the premises are considered true, the argument is valid.

This argument happens to be comprised of truthful statements. But although it might seem counterintuitive at first, an argument can be perfectly valid without containing a single statement that is factually correct. That's because validity is completely independent of **truth values**. To illustrate this point, we can alter the preceding argument so that it remains valid but no longer contains any true statements.

1. All bananas are purple.
2. Socrates is a banana.
3. Therefore, Socrates is purple.

Despite the fact that its content is completely nonsensical, this argument is perfectly valid, in logical terms. That's because if we assume that the premises are true, the conclusion *must* also be true. When we test for validity, we consider the content of each statement only in terms of its relationship to the other parts of the argument, asking if the truth of the premises would necessitate the truth of the conclusion. Validity is entirely determined by the argument's structure, with no regard to its meaning.

In fact, when we test for validity, we can rephrase deductive arguments as simple formulas and achieve the same results.

1. All bananas are purple.	1. All B are P.
2. Socrates is a banana.	2. S is a B.
3. Therefore, Socrates is purple.	3. Therefore, S is P.

Now that we've stripped the argument down to its most basic form, it's easy to see how even the most ridiculous argument can be valid if it has the right structure; it must simply be designed in such a way that if its premises are asserted to be true, it will not make sense to deny its conclusion.

So far, we've discussed examples of arguments that are valid. However, it's just as important to know what invalid arguments look like. We'll discuss invalid arguments at greater length when we discuss deductive fallacies in a later chapter. For now, let's look at a simple example of an argument in which the premises do not necessitate the conclusion.

1. Socrates is purple.
2. All bananas are purple.
3. Therefore, Socrates is a banana.

In this example, we have an argument of the form

1. S is P.
2. All B are P.
3. Therefore, S is a B.

Clearly, the premises in this argument do not necessitate the conclusion. Even if Socrates were purple and bananas were also purple, these facts would not make Socrates a banana. After all, based on the limited information available, he could just as easily be a grape, an eggplant, or a starfish.

Testing for validity is an important first step in analyzing a deductive argument. Keep in mind, however, that validity is only a test of the basic framework of the argument, and that, while an invalid argument might damage a writer's credibility, passing the validity test does not indicate that an argument contains any more truth than the argument that Socrates is a purple banana.

Soundness

The truth of an argument's premises finally comes into play when we are determining whether an argument is sound.

In order to be sound, in logical terms, an argument must be valid. If the argument is valid and has premises that are all true, it is also sound.

The following is an example of a sound argument.

1. There are twelve inches in a foot.
2. There are three feet in a yard.
3. Therefore, there are thirty-six inches in a yard.

As you can see, the structure of this argument is valid (i.e., the conclusion is necessitated by the premises). The argument is also sound because, in addition to having a valid form, the argument also has premises that are true.

By extension of this rule, an *invalid* argument whose premises are true will always be *unsound*. The following argument provides an example.

Soundness Test: A valid argument whose premises are all true is considered sound.

Invalid,
Unsound

1. All wombats are mortal.	True premise
2. Socrates is a man.	True premise
3. Therefore, Socrates is mortal.	True conclusion

This argument is composed of true statements, but because the argument is not valid, it cannot be considered sound.

Likewise, a valid argument whose premises are not *all* true cannot be sound.

Valid,
Unsound

1. Socrates is a wombat.	False premise
2. All wombats are mortal.	True premise
3. Therefore, Socrates is mortal.	True conclusion

This argument is valid because the conclusion follows logically from the premises. Nevertheless, the fact that the first premise is false makes this argument unsound.

Exercise 1: Identification

Match each term with the appropriate description below. There is only one correct response for each item.

> **soundness, validity, deductive argument,
> syllogism, inductive argument**

1. Conclusion speculates about possibilities suggested by the premises; said to move from specific to general.

2. Test for proper form: the conclusion *must* be true if the premises are true.

3. Major premise: All birds have wings.
   Minor premise: All parrots are birds.
   Conclusion: Therefore, all parrots have wings.

4. Test for proper form *and* true premises.

5. Conclusion is a logical consequence of the premises; said to progress from general to specific.

Exercise 2: Explanation

Each of the following arguments is unsound. Explain why each argument is unsound by identifying its form as valid or invalid and its premises as true, untrue, or indeterminate (if the truth value cannot be determined).

1. All deductive arguments are valid.
   This is a deductive argument.
   Therefore, this argument is valid.

2. All men are mortal.
   Socrates is mortal.
   Therefore, Socrates is a man.

3. All doctors have degrees.
   Fred has a degree.
   Therefore, Fred is a doctor.

Exercise 3: Imitation

Create an example of a sound argument, and explain why it is sound. Then, alter your argument in a way that renders it unsound, and explain why it is no longer sound.

Exercise 4: Evaluation

For each of the following arguments, identify the type of reasoning employed as deductive or inductive, and explain your answer. If the argument is deductive, explain what makes the argument valid or invalid.

1. A study has shown that the death penalty is not an effective deterrent against violent crimes. The study reports a decrease in the incidence of murders in Utopia since the nation outlawed the death penalty in 1987. Based on this data, researchers have concluded that the same would be true in other nations if they were to eradicate the practice of capital punishment.

2. The cook was murdered in the kitchen with a candlestick at midnight. If Professor Plum was not in the kitchen at the time of the murder, he could not have committed the crime. Professor Plum was spotted at the local Wal-Mart at midnight on the night of the murder. Therefore, Professor Plum could not have murdered the cook.

Analyzing Inductive Arguments

Induction in Real Life

Outside of academic settings, people usually express their arguments in a casual manner. To understand what inductive arguments often look like in real life, let's take a look at how an argument of the kind found in textbooks might translate to ordinary speech.

Example:
1. I have seen many swans.
2. All the swans I've seen have been white.
3. Therefore, all swans are probably white.

Ordinary Speech:
"Based on my experience, I think all swans are white."

In this example, "based on my experience" implies that the speaker has seen swans and that they have all been white (premises one and two), but neither premise is explicitly stated.

Now, let's consider a possible counterargument.

Example:
1. I read on the Internet that some swans are black.
2. Therefore, it is probably not true that all swans are white.

Ordinary Speech:
"I've read that there are black swans."

Even with only one premise, this argument can still be abbreviated even further in common speech. In this example, the argument is reduced from two statements to one. Here, it is the conclusion that goes unspoken. The speaker is clearly arguing against the idea that all swans are white, but leaves it up to the audience to make that connection.

Evaluating Inductive Reasoning

Like deductive arguments, inductive arguments can be assessed using a specific set of rules. Armed with an understanding of these principles, we are better prepared to dismantle the fallacious arguments we are exposed to and recognize our own errors in reasoning.

In the previous chapter, we discussed the concepts of validity and soundness, which are used to measure the effectiveness of deductive arguments. When we're working with *inductive* arguments, we use the terms **strength** and **cogency**. There is a rough correspondence between the two sets of terms, but there are also significant differences that reflect the unique natures of inductive and deductive reasoning.

Strength

Strength is a measure of the degree to which the premises of an argument suggest its conclusion. The concept of strength is similar to the idea of validity, in that both concepts measure the relationship between an argument's premises and its conclusion.

When we measure validity in deductive reasoning, an argument's conclusion must be a definite logical consequence of its premises in order to be considered valid. By contrast, an inductive argument's premises must render a given conclusion *probable* in order for the argument to be considered strong.

Example:
1. My computer has been stolen.
2. Melissa is the only other person who has a key to my office.
3. Therefore, Melissa probably stole my computer.

In this argument, the premises render it highly likely that the conclusion is true. Although it's still conceivable that if both premises are true, the conclusion might be false, this argument is inductively strong. That's because the purpose of an inductive argument is not to prove that its conclusion must be true beyond any doubt. Rather, a strong inductive argument merely proposes an explanation that is *probably* true in light of the available evidence, which in this case is the fact that Melissa possesses the only other key to the office. While a deductive argument must have premises that definitively prove its conclusion in order to be valid, an inductive argument is considered strong if its premises suggest that its conclusion is merely likely to be true. This is one of the major differences between validity and strength.

Strength Test: An inductive argument is considered strong if the truth of its premises would compellingly suggest the truth of its conclusion.

Another difference between tests of validity and strength is the fact that strength is measured in degrees. While a deductive argument is either valid or invalid, an inductive argument can be strong, weak, or something in between. Testing for inductive strength is a subjective process.

Keep in mind that even an exceptionally strong inductive argument will not prove its conclusion with absolute certainty, as a valid deductive argument would do. Inductive arguments involve some degree of uncertainty and speculation.

Looking at examples of weaker arguments can give us a better idea of what is meant by "strength." In the following inductive argument, the premises do not suggest the conclusion at all.

Example:
1. Grass is green.
2. Spinach is green.
3. Spinach and grass probably taste the same.

Like validity, the strength of an argument is determined without regard to the truth or falsity of the claims the argument makes. For example, the following argument is weak, even though its premises are true.

1. Grass is green.	True
2. Spinach is green.	True
3. Spinach and grass probably taste the same.	Not probable based on the premises.

However, while strength does not depend on the truth of the premises, it does depend on their content. While we could test for validity by simply reducing arguments into formulas, paying no attention to the meanings of the terms we were using, the same is not true when we test the strength of an inductive argument, as the preceding example illustrates.

An argument that is neither very strong nor especially weak will fall somewhere in the middle of the continuum. The following is an example of such an argument:

1. Most lights in the night sky are stars.
2. I just saw a light in the night sky.
3. The light I saw must have been a star.

In this argument, if we assume that the premises are true, the conclusion might also be true, but there is significant room for doubt. The light the speaker refers to in the second premise might have been created by a satellite, an airplane, a comet, the moon, or by a distant planet.

Cogency

An argument is considered cogent if it is strong and has premises that are all true. The concept of cogency in inductive reasoning is similar to that of soundness in deductive thought; both concepts take into account not only the relationship between the premises and conclusion, but also the truth value of the premises.

The following is an example of a cogent inductive argument:

1. On average, women are shorter than men.
2. There are fifty men and fifty women in this room.
3. If the heights of each group are averaged, the men will probably have a greater average height than the women.

As you can see, the structure of the argument is strong because if its premises are true, its conclusion is also likely to be true. Since the argument also consists of all true premises, it would also be classified as cogent.

By definition, a weak argument whose premises are all true cannot be cogent. The following example illustrates what a weak argument with true premises would look like:

1. Some parrots can speak.
2. My sister Amanda can speak.
3. My sister Amanda is a parrot.

Likewise, a strong argument whose premises are *not* all true cannot be cogent.

Cogency Test: A strong inductive argument whose premises are all true is considered cogent.

1. The average human body temperature is 55° F.
2. My current temperature is 102° F.
3. I probably have a fever.

In this example, the conclusion is rendered probable by the second premise; if a person's body temperature is 102° F, the individual most likely has a fever. Nevertheless, the fact that the first premise is false makes it impossible for this argument to be considered cogent.

Exercise 1: Identification

Match each term with the appropriate description below. There is only one correct response for each item.

> ## deductive, strong, sound, inductive, valid, cogent

1. The conclusion of this kind of argument is a logical consequence of its premises, and the premises are all true.

2. A deductive argument that has a proper form, but which may or may not contain true premises.

3. This kind of argument is strong, and all of its premises are true.

4. An argument that can be evaluated in terms of validity and soundness.

5. This kind of argument is not meant to prove definitively that its conclusion is true; it merely proves that the conclusion is probably true.

6. In this argument, it's very likely that the conclusion is true if the premises are true.

Exercise 2: Explanation

The following arguments may be either strong or weak. For each, choose one of these two designations, and explain your answer.

1. Peter and his pet, Rover, both have canine teeth.
   The word "canine" means "dog."
   Therefore, Peter and Rover are both dogs.

2. Alice is going to the emergency room because she has fractured her toe.
   Bone fractures are almost always painful.
   Therefore, Alice is in pain.

3. Melinda and her pet canary can both sing.
   Melinda uses her vocal chords to sing.
   Therefore, the canary also has vocal chords.

Exercise 3: Imitation

Create an example of a cogent argument, and explain why it is cogent. Then, alter your argument in a way that renders it no longer cogent.

Exercise 4: Evaluation

For each of the following arguments, identify the type of reasoning employed as deductive or inductive, and explain your answer. If the argument is inductive, describe the argument as weak or strong, and explain your decision.

1. The word "obtuse" means stupid or dull-witted. The word "abstruse" means technical, mysterious, or profound. When Alicia said that Einstein's theory of relativity was "intellectual and obtuse," she contradicted herself; the term "abstruse" would have been more accurate.

2. When you said that Einstein's theory of relativity was "intellectual and obtuse," you contradicted yourself. People often confuse the terms "obtuse" and "abstruse" because they sound similar. You probably meant to say that it was "abstruse."

Logical Fallacies

"No one who lives in error is free."

EURIPIDES

Logical Fallacies

THE WORD "FALLACY" MEANS "error." This term is often used as a synonym for the word "myth," to describe a popular but incorrect belief.

A **logical fallacy** is a specific kind of error—a mistake in reasoning. This kind of fallacy occurs when an argument contains a mistake that makes it invalid (for a deductive argument) or weak (for an inductive argument). In this book, the term "fallacy" is used to refer specifically to a *logical* fallacy.[11]

Formal and Informal Fallacies

There are two main categories of logical errors: **formal fallacies** and **informal fallacies**.

The term "formal" refers to the structure of an argument and the branch of logic that is most concerned with structure—deductive reasoning. All formal fallacies are errors in deductive reasoning that render an argument invalid. The term "informal" refers to the non-structural aspects of arguments, usually emphasized in inductive reasoning. *Most* informal fallacies are errors of induction, but some of these fallacies can apply to deductive arguments as well.

In the next chapter, we'll discuss the basic characteristics of formal fallacies. After that, we'll talk about a few of the most common informal fallacies that are found in everyday use.

Formal fallacies are mistakes in deductive reasoning that render an argument's form invalid.

Informal fallacies, generally found in inductive arguments, are non-structural errors that make an argument weak.

---

[11] The term "logical fallacy" is sometimes used to refer to formal (i.e., deductive) fallacies only. In this book, however, we use the term to refer to both formal and informal errors of reasoning. This is a useful and commonly accepted way of distinguishing mistakes in the reasoning process (i.e., logical fallacies) from factual errors.

Formal Fallacies

Formal fallacies are errors in deduction. While deductive arguments may not play as pronounced a role in daily life as inductive arguments do, it's important to be able to recognize formal fallacies wherever they occur. Being prepared to recognize and refute erroneous thinking is essential to making good decisions, presenting a strong ethos, and expressing ideas effectively.

The first step to recognizing formal fallacies is to understand what they are. Put simply, formal fallacies are invalid forms of deductive arguments.

There are many kinds of formal fallacies. Fortunately, you'll only need to remember one name in order to identify any formal fallacy because the term **non sequitur** describes any deductive argument that has a flawed structure. In the following chapter, we'll learn more about formal fallacies, including methods for identifying and refuting non sequitur arguments.

Non Sequitur:

It *"does not follow," logically.*

The Latin term "non sequitur" can be translated literally as, "it does not follow." In logic, this expression describes an argument in which the conclusion does not logically follow from the premises. This fallacy has nothing to do with the chronological sequence of events; instead, it's about the logical progression of ideas.

Etymology: The word "sequitur" shares a common root with the words "sequence" and "sequel," which also convey the idea of one thing following another.

Premises → **Conclusion**

A non sequitur is a deductive argument in which the conclusion "does not follow" inevitably from the premises. All invalid deductive arguments can be said to commit the non sequitur fallacy.

Example:
1. All aardvarks are mammals.
2. All mammals are animals.
3. Therefore, all animals are aardvarks.

In this example, we can identify the argument as *invalid* because the premises do not logically necessitate the conclusion. In other words, the conclusion "does not follow" from the premises. Because it is invalid—because its *form* is flawed—this kind of argument is said to commit a "formal" fallacy. And because it commits a formal fallacy, we can describe it using the term "non sequitur."

Non sequitur arguments can take a variety of forms, and they may or may not contain true statements. Here's an example of an argument whose premises are true.

1. Socrates is Greek. (S is G.)
2. Some men are Greek. (Some M are G.)
3. Therefore, Socrates is a man. (S is an M.)

The one identifying feature of an argument that commits this fallacy is the fact that the argument is clearly deductive, but it is not valid—the truth of its premises does not logically require the truth of its conclusion. In the previous argument, for example, although Socrates is indeed Greek, and although some men are Greek, these facts do not necessitate the conclusion (which happens to be true) that Socrates is a man. Based on the premises in this argument, he could just as easily be a Greek olive, the Parthenon, or the city of Athens.

Outside the discipline of logic, the term "non sequitur" is also used to refer to a comedic device in which the speaker connects seemingly random ideas. In this line from the 1930 movie *Animal Crackers*, Groucho Marx[12] delivers an example of a humorous non sequitur.

> *Well, Art is Art, isn't it? Still, on the other hand, water is water. And east is east and west is west and if you take cranberries and stew them like applesauce, they taste much more like prunes than rhubarb does. Now you tell me what you know.*

This speech is funny in part because it mimics the non sequitur style of reasoning. Groucho connects his observations as one might connect premises in an argument. But, as anyone can see, his thoughts are completely disjointed and prove nothing.

Unlike this argument, which is intended to be humorous, most non sequitur arguments you'll encounter in real life are subtle and difficult to detect. The simplest way to identify a non sequitur argument is to first evaluate whether the argument is deductive—claiming that its premises prove its conclusion with absolute certainty— and then determine whether the premises actually leave room for doubt.

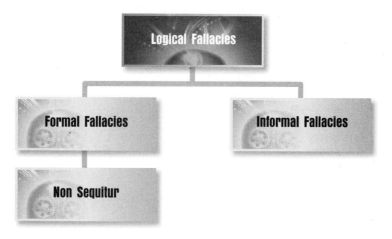

---

[12] Stage name of comedian Julius Henry Marx

Exercise 1: Identification

Identify each of the following as an example of either a valid argument or a non sequi-tur fallacy. Keep in mind that the validity of the argument is not related to the truth or falsity of the argument's premises or conclusion; an argument is valid or fallacious based only on its form.

1. If there is water on Mars, then there must also be life on Mars.
   There is water on Mars.
   Therefore, there is life on Mars.

2. If an NFC team wins the Super Bowl, then the stock market will go up.
   The stock market has gone up.
   Therefore, an NFC team has won the Super Bowl.

3. If an animal is a rodent, then it will have prominent incisor teeth.
   Rabbits have prominent incisor teeth.
   Therefore, rabbits are rodents.

4. If the water in the kettle reaches 100° C, then it will boil.
   The water has reached 100° C.
   Therefore, the water is boiling.

Exercise 2: Explanation

Each of the following arguments commits a non sequitur fallacy. Identify what makes the argument invalid.

1. Giant pandas have black fur.
   Therefore, giant pandas do not have white fur.

2. If I get a promotion, then the sky will be blue.
   I did not get a promotion.
   Therefore, the sky is not blue.

Exercise 3: Imitation

Create an example of a valid deductive argument. Then, convert your original argument into a non sequitur fallacy. Explain the difference between the valid argument and the fallacious argument.

Example of a valid argument:
> All hobbits are short.
> Frodo is a hobbit.
> Therefore, Frodo is short.

Example of a non sequitur fallacy:
> All hobbits are short.
> Sam is short.
> Therefore, Sam is a hobbit.

Explanation: In the first argument, the premises prove the conclusion without leaving any room for doubt. If it is true that all hobbits are short and that Frodo is a hobbit, then it must be true that Frodo is short. In the second argument, however, it is possible for the conclusion to be false. Even if all hobbits are short, and Sam is short, it is still possible that Sam is not a hobbit.

Exercise 4: Evaluation

The following passage is an excerpt from Abraham Lincoln's "Fragment on Slavery," dated July 1, 1854. In this deductive argument, Lincoln discusses one factor that was often used to justify slavery in the United States: differences in skin color. Read the passage carefully. Then, restate the argument in your own words. Finally, determine whether the argument is a valid deductive argument or an example of the non sequitur fallacy. Explain your answer.

If A. can prove, however conclusively, that he may, of right, enslave B.—why may not B. snatch the same argument, and prove equally, that he may enslave A? You say A. is white, and B. is black. It is color, then; the lighter, having the right to enslave the darker? Take care. By this rule, you are to be slave to the first man you meet, with a fairer skin than your own.

Informal Fallacies

Informal fallacies are everywhere, and learning to recognize and refute them—and to avoid committing them ourselves—is an essential part of becoming an effective thinker and communicator.

The simplest way to define informal fallacies is to contrast them with their formal counterparts. First, while formal fallacies are purely a matter of invalid form, informal fallacies are content-level errors. This difference is the source of the names "formal" and "informal." Most informal fallacies are inductive errors, although there are several that can be committed in deductive arguments as well. While formal fallacies are mistakes that render a deductive argument invalid, most informal fallacies are usually errors that make an inductive argument weak.

As we discussed in the chapter on inductive reasoning, determining whether an argument is strong or weak is a somewhat subjective process. By learning about the specific kinds of informal fallacies, we can learn which patterns of inductive reasoning are universally considered weak.

There are many varieties of informal fallacies, but the fallacies that follow are some of the most common.[13]

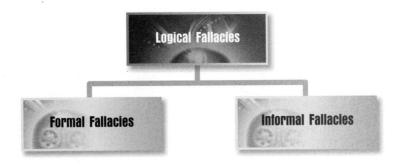

---

[13] Many of these fallacies have also been mentioned in the AP Language and Composition Exam.

Non Causa Pro Causa:

Correlation does not prove causation.

Non causa pro causa is the fallacy of mistaken causation. The fallacy's Latin name translates to "non-cause for cause." Alternative names for this kind of fallacy include "false cause" and "questionable cause." As each of these names suggests, the non causa fallacy takes place when an argument treats a factor that is not a cause (i.e., a "non-cause") as a cause.

> *Aliases Include:*
> • **False Cause**
> • **Questionable Cause**
>
> *Sub-Fallacies Include:*
> • **Cum Hoc, Ergo Propter Hoc**
> • **Post Hoc, Ergo Propter Hoc**

Often, non causa arguments mistake mere coincidence or **correlation** for **causation**.

> **correlation**: the relationship between two factors. Example: "The increase in temperature was correlated with a simultaneous increase in gas prices."

> **causation**: the act of producing an effect. Example: "Falling down the stairs caused Jennifer to break her arm."

A well-reasoned argument will not treat correlation as definitive proof of causation. Even if different factors appear to be related in some way, one cannot assume that there is any kind of cause-and-effect relationship between them without evidence that shows direct causation.

Non causa arguments often fail because they overlook the possibility that two factors may be related by mere chance; they presume that if two factors appear to be related in some way (e.g., by occurring at the same time), the relationship must be of a cause-effect nature. However, this is not always the case. The following argument commits this fallacy.

1. My grandmother lived to the age of 98.
2. My grandmother ate chocolate every day.
3. My grandmother lived to the age of 98 *because she ate chocolate every day*.

In this argument, the speaker assumes that there is a direct causal relationship between the grandmother's longevity and her sweet tooth. In reality, these two factors may be completely unrelated, but the argument wrongly assumes that they bear specific cause-and-effect relationship to one another (i.e., that eating chocolate caused the grandmother to live a long life).

Keep in mind that it's possible to draw an incorrect conclusion about causality without committing the non causa pro causa fallacy. In inductive reasoning, it's possible to come to a false conclusion even if your reasoning is strong. Likewise, it's possible to come up with a conclusion that's factually correct using an illogical, non causa argument. You can identify a non causa argument by its insistence on a specific cause-effect relationship using inadequate premises.

There are several subcategories of non causa pro causa arguments, and in the following pages, we'll briefly explore two of the more commonly seen varieties—***cum hoc, ergo propter hoc*** and ***post hoc, ergo propter hoc***:

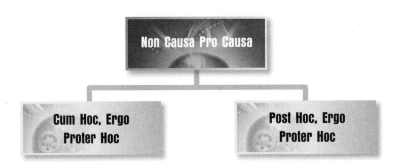

Cum Hoc, Ergo Propter Hoc:
Concurrence does not prove consequence.

The Latin phrase "cum hoc, ergo propter hoc" translates to "with this, therefore because of this." It describes a situation in which a speaker assumes there is a causal relationship between two factors simply because they occur at the same time. But, as we will discuss, the fact that two events happen simultaneously does not necessarily mean that they share a cause-and-effect relationship.

In the previous discussion of non causa pro causa fallacies, the argument about the grandmother who ate chocolate every day was an example of a cum hoc, ergo propter hoc argument. For another example of an argument that commits the cum hoc fallacy, consider the following imaginary scenario.

> *An organization called the Society for a Bread-Free Nation (SBFN) cites the following facts in its mission statement: "In the 18ᵗʰ century, when virtually all bread was baked in the home, the average life expectancy was less than 50 years; infant mortality rates were unacceptably high; many women died in childbirth; and diseases such as typhoid, yellow fever, and influenza ravaged whole nations." On the basis of these facts, the society argues that baking bread is a dangerous activity that poses serious health risks. Therefore, they propose strict government regulation of the bread-making industry and a ban on making bread in the home.*

In this scenario, the SBFN mistakes concurrence for causation. The argument is obviously absurd, and in such situations, it's easy to recognize the error inherent in cum hoc fallacies.

Unfortunately, it is often far more difficult to recognize such fallacies when the argument seems more plausible, and we frequently encounter similarly flawed arguments without thinking twice before accepting them. Here's a more realistic example of a cum hoc argument you might encounter.

Scientists confirm link between ADD and cell phones

Studies have shown that since the use of cell phones has become more widespread worldwide, diagnoses of Attention Deficit Disorder (ADD) have increased dramatically. These findings seem to suggest that the radiation emitted by cell phones may cause ADD in some users.

To combat this kind of argument, remember to ask whether the simultaneous occurrence of A and B means that A caused B. Being mindful of the weakness of this kind of argument can prevent you from making many mistakes in reasoning.

Post Hoc, Ergo Propter Hoc:
Subsequence does not prove consequence.

The post hoc, ergo propter hoc fallacy is one of the most common types of fallacies you'll come across, and it is closely related to the cum hoc fallacy. The Latin phrase *post hoc, ergo propter hoc* means "after this, therefore because of this." As you may have guessed, the post hoc fallacy occurs when a speaker attempts to argue that one thing has caused another using only the chronological sequence of events as evidence. The event that happens first is assumed to have caused the event that follows.

For an example of what these kinds of fallacies look like, let's consider another argument from the Society for a Bread-Free Nation.

> *The Society for a Bread-Free Nation claims that more than 90 percent of violent crimes are committed within 24 hours after the perpetrator has eaten bread. These findings seem to suggest that consuming bread inspires violent behavior.*

If a person commits a violent crime within 24 hours of eating bread, does that mean that eating bread *caused* the individual to behave violently? The obvious answer is no: the consumption of bread cannot be linked to the incidence of violent crimes, based on this information alone. Many people, if not most, consume bread on a daily basis without committing acts of violence. If there were significant further evidence of a connection between bread consumption and crime, SBFN might be able to make the case that eating bread causes violence, but without further proof, their argument is extremely weak.

For a more realistic example, consider the following argument, similar to one you might hear in a news-analysis program:

Since the new president has been in office, the federal budget deficit has decreased by ten percent, and unemployment has decreased by an average of four percent, nationwide. These changes clearly show that the current president has improved the nation's economy.

This argument might sound stronger than the argument linking bread to violence, but it uses the same fallacious reasoning. With the limited information the speaker presents, we are left asking essentially the same question we asked in the previous scenario: does the fact that A occurred before B prove that A *caused* B? The answer, of course, is no. While the information about changes in the budget deficit and unemployment rates could be used to support a more detailed argument about the effects of a president's specific policies, this information does not in itself "clearly show that the current president has improved the nation's economy," as the speaker claims.

As with the cum hoc fallacy, the best way to refute post hoc arguments is to simply point out the fact that a chronological relationship between two events does not mean that one caused the other.

Exercise 1: Identification

Identify each of the following arguments as either a sound argument or an example of a non causa pro causa fallacy.

1. Our company's stock prices plummeted on June 19th.
   We hired a new intern that day.
   Stock prices fell because we hired the intern.

2. I took antibiotics yesterday.
   I've been feeling sick today.
   The antibiotics have made me feel sick.

3. Yesterday, I saw a stray cat in my yard.
   I have never seen any other cat in my yard.
   Today, I found paw prints in my yard that look like they were made by a cat.
   The stray cat probably created the paw prints I found in my yard.

Exercise 2: Explanation

Each of the following arguments commits a kind of non causa pro causa fallacy. For each argument, identify the fallacy that's being committed as an instance of either cum hoc, post hoc, or simply another form of non causa pro causa. Explain your answer.

1. A study by the research branch of the International Institute for Paper Cut Awareness showed that of all the age-groups polled, people who were 25-35 years old seem to have the highest incidence of paper cuts, proving conclusively that this is a high-risk age group.

2. Of those surveyed, 27% of current paper cut sufferers were also found to be currently suffering from chronic sleep disturbances. This confirms the theory that sleep disturbances are a symptom of paper cuts.

3. The study also proved the link between paper cuts and driving, demonstrating that for those of driving age, over 86% of paper cuts are inflicted less than four hours after the sufferer has operated a vehicle. Researchers believe this clearly demonstrates that driving is a major cause of paper cuts.

Exercise 3: Imitation

Create an example of either a cum hoc or a post hoc argument. Identify which type of fallacy you are illustrating, and explain why the argument is weak.

Exercise 4: Evaluation

The following quote comes from an article titled "Spanking Causes Aggression in Children," published by XYZ News. Read the passage carefully. Then, determine whether the argument contained in this quote is strong or fallacious. If the argument is strong, explain why. If it is weak, identify which fallacy is contained in the quote, and explain what information the article would need to contain in order to make a strong argument for causation.

"Children who are spanked when they are five years old are more likely to behave aggressively at the age of seven than they otherwise would have, a new study suggests. Those children who had been spanked were 50% more likely to use physical aggression, name-calling, and talk back to their parents than were their non-spanked peers, according to researchers at The University of Okoboji in Iowa."

Weak Analogy:

Comparing apples and oranges

One of the simplest forms of inductive reasoning is the **argument by analogy**. This kind of argument makes the claim that since two items have a given attribute in common, they must also share a second, distinct point of similarity. In other words, arguments by analogy assert that

1. A is like B.
2. B has property X.
3. Therefore, A also has property X.

> *Aliases Include:*
> - **False Analogy**
> - **Faulty Analogy**

This is the underlying form that all analogies share. But arguments that are based on analogies are rarely expressed so directly, with explicit statements of comparison and a definitive conclusion. More often, arguments by analogy are presented in a simplified form. For example, the well-known adage "the squeaky wheel gets the grease" is a shorthand form of the following argument:

1. A person who complains loudly and frequently attracts attention, just as a squeaky wheel does.
2. Squeaky wheels get the service they need because they attract attention to themselves.
3. Therefore, people who complain loudly are also more likely to get the service they need.

As illustrated here, even a comparison between such dissimilar items as a human being and a wheel can create a surprisingly persuasive **analogy**. Despite the many differences between human beings and wheels, both are often more likely to receive what they desire when they attract attention to themselves.

As this example illustrates, analogies often make strange and unexpected comparisons, resulting in memorable, and often entertaining, illustrations. However, in some analogies, the differences between the objects of comparison are more than merely funny or odd—sometimes they are so significant that they actually defeat the argument. In such cases, when the comparison between A and B does not lead to the conclusion given, we have a fallacy known as a **weak analogy**.

For a literary example of a weak analogy, consider the following dialogue from Mark Twain's *Adventures of Huckleberry Finn*. In this passage, Huck proposes an analogy (in the bolded passage), and Jim finds fault with the argument.

> "S'pose a man was to come to you and say Polly-voo-franzy—what would you think?"
>
> "I wouldn' think nuff'n; I'd take en bust him over de head . . . ."
>
> "Shucks . . . It's only saying, do you know how to talk French?"

"Well, den, why couldn't he say it?"

"Why, he *is* a-saying it. That's a Frenchman's way of saying it."

"Well, it's a blame ridicklous way, en I doan' want to hear no mo' 'bout it. Dey ain' no sense in it."

"Looky here, Jim; does a cat talk like we do?"

"No, a cat don't."

"Well, does a cow?"

"No, a cow don't, nuther."

"Does a cat talk like a cow, or a cow talk like a cat?"

"No, dey don't."

"It's natural and right for 'em to talk different from each other, ain't it?"

"Course."

"And ain't it natural and right for a cat and a cow to talk different from us?"

"Why, mos' sholy it is."

"Well, then, why ain't it natural and right for a Frenchman to talk different from us? You answer me that."

In this example, Huck makes the following argument:

1. The variation between people of different nationalities—in this case, French and American—is similar to the variation between animals of different species.
2. Animals of different species do not make the same sounds or communicate in the same way.
3. Therefore, it is natural that humans of different nationalities should not speak the same language.

Here, Huck's conclusion—that it is natural for people of different nationalities to speak different languages—is correct. Nevertheless, his argument is fallacious because it is based on a weak analogy. Huck equates nationality with species as a means of explaining linguistic differences. Now, let's look at Jim's response to Huck's analogy.

"Is a cat a man, Huck?"

"No."

"Well, den, dey ain't no sense in a cat talkin' like a man. Is a cow a man? —er is a cow a cat?"

"No, she ain't either of them."

"Well, den, she ain't got no business to talk like either one er the yuther of 'em. Is a Frenchman a man?"

"Yes."

"*Well*, den! Dad blame it, why doan' he talk like a man? You answer me *dat*!"

As Jim points out, the differences between species are not analogous to the differences among different groups of people. In this passage, Jim provides an example of how an argument that is based on a weak analogy can be refuted. By pointing out that cats and cows are not of the same species, Jim illustrates the fact that Huck's analogy is seriously flawed.

If there is at least one specific, fundamental difference between the objects of an analogy that casts doubt on the argument's conclusion, the argument can probably be called weak. No analogy is perfect, and among legitimate analogies, some are stronger and more effective than others. For example, let's take another look at the analogy we discussed earlier about the squeaky wheel. The strength of the argument "the squeaky wheel gets the grease" depends on the context in which it is used. If someone were to use this expression to convince you to yell "fire" in a crowded theater, the analogy would obviously be quite weak. However, if used to explain why the employee who complained about her pay received the highest raise, the analogy would be rather strong.

Unfortunately, most weak analogies do not contain obvious flaws. Assessing the strength of an analogy usually takes careful analysis. When analyzing an analogy, remember to look for differences between the two items or situations that are being compared, and see if any of these differences significantly diminish the strength of the argument.

A common idiom used for objecting to a weak analogy is the expression "comparing apples and oranges." The full argument in this analogy can be spelled out as follows:

1. Comparing objects A and B is like comparing apples and oranges.
2. It is unreasonable to compare apples and oranges because they belong in different categories.
3. Therefore, it is also unreasonable to compare objects A and B.

While most legitimate analogies do compare unlike things, such as apples and oranges, this saying succinctly expresses the importance of comparing objects that can legitimately be equated in the context of the argument. When you are confronted with an analogy, this saying should remind you that the comparison may be unreasonable based on the differences between the objects involved.

Hasty Generalization:
Haste makes waste.

The fallacy of **hasty generalization** is a type of weak analogy in which the speaker draws a conclusion based on an unrepresentative sample. In this subtype of the false-analogy fallacy, the speaker makes an analogy between a part and the whole, but the part does not truly exemplify the whole. Let's look at an example of this kind of analogy.

Example:
1. Chester is a cat.
2. Chester has no tail.
3. Therefore, cats have no tails.

This argument is weak because it makes an assumption about all cats based on a very small sample group: a single cat named Chester. Any argument that commits the hasty-generalization fallacy will follow the same basic formula:

1. A is part of B.	(Chester is a cat.)
2. A has quality X.	(Chester has no tail.)
3. Therefore, B also has quality X.	(Therefore, cats have no tails.)

For the sake of illustration, let's consider an extreme example: a political pollster predicts the outcome of a presidential election based on a poll of ten randomly selected individuals. The sample group of ten individuals is then treated as analogous to the entire voting population. Based on the fact that four respondents said they would vote for Mickey Mouse and six claimed they would vote for Donald Duck, the pollster argues that Mr. Mouse will receive 40% of the votes, while Mr. Duck will win the election with 60%. In other words:

1. The ten individuals who were polled represent the entire population of the United States.
2. The group voted 6:4 in favor of Donald Duck.
3. Therefore, the American people will vote 6:4 in favor of Donald Duck.

Clearly, such a poll would not be scientifically meaningful because the first premise of the argument—the idea that the ten people who were surveyed accurately represent the entire population of the country—is very weak. A hasty generalization like this one might correctly predict future outcomes once in a while, but only by random coincidence.

Of course, it's not always unreasonable to draw conclusions based on a small sample. Under the right conditions, it makes sense to make an analogy between a small part and the whole—and often, there is no other option. With the proper use of statistical methods, we can make predictions that have some inductive value. Unlike the pollster in the example we used earlier, professional pollsters make generalizations based on samples that have been carefully chosen to represent the entire population, based on scientific principles.

Fortunately, it's not necessary to become a professional statistician in order to make reasonable generalizations in more casual situations. For instance, it's perfectly reasonable to draw a conclusion about the quality of a batch of chocolate-chip cookies after only a few bites; one need not eat the entire batch to determine whether they all taste good. If the cookies are made from the same batter and are baked for the same amount of time at a uniform temperature—in other words, if the group in question can be assumed to be relatively homogeneous—the sample group can be considered truly representative of the whole, and a generalization can reasonably be made from a small sample. By contrast, tasting only one chocolate-chip cookie and drawing conclusions about a tray of chocolate-chip, oatmeal, sugar, and pecan cookies based on this small sample would be a hasty generalization.

When assessing a generalization that might be fallacious, it's best to do what we would do with any other suspicious analogy: look for differences between the two objects of comparison. In the case of generalizations, we compare the sample (e.g., the people polled or the cookie tasted) and the whole (e.g., the entire population of voters or the whole batch of cookies). If the sample is significantly different from the whole, whether by virtue of size, composition, or any other factor that could damage the analogy, we must view the argument as a hasty generalization.

Stereotypes: *They're all the same to me.*

One common form of hasty generalization is the ***stereotype***—a widely accepted, simplistic view of people who belong to a given group. In addition to being a form of cognitive bias, stereotyping is also a fallacious technique used in argumentation. Like other hasty generalizations, arguments based on stereotypes make unmerited assumptions about a large group based on a small sample.

Stereotypes usually deal specifically with people. They characterize everyone who shares a particular quality—whether it be an ethnicity, a profession, or a shoe size—as sharing some other trait or group of traits. These generalizations can be positive or negative, but most of the views that we categorize as stereotypes have been accepted by a large group of people.

For example, you might hear an argument like the following:

> *I've known many politicians, and you can't trust any of them; they're all liars.*

Or, in common speech, the speaker might simply say, "all politicians are liars." In this stereotype, the speaker makes an assumption about every member of a large group of people (politicians) based on personal experiences or hearsay. To put it in more formal terms,

The term "stereotype" comes from the Greek words stereos, meaning "solid," and typos, which means "impression" or "mark." The word was originally used to describe a printing process in which metal plates were used to mass-produce publications. In 1922, journalist Walter Lippmann borrowed this imagery to describe the phenomenon in which people make hasty generalizations about entire groups of people based on preconceptions or limited experiences. Just as printers mass-produced identical images from a single metal plate, the human mind tends to impose preconceived notions on entire groups of people.

1. All the politicians I have known (or heard about) have been liars.
2. All politicians are exactly like the politicians I have known (or heard about).
3. Therefore, all politicians are liars.

While this particular generalization is not particularly controversial and is often met with little objection, it is, nonetheless, a fallacious argument. To illustrate just how weak this line of reasoning is, let's look at another argument of the same form that discusses a different subject.

You can't trust left-handed people; they're all liars.

Although this argument does not express a commonly held view, it is based on the same assumptions that were found in the previous argument:

1. A seems to have quality X.
2. A is perfectly representative of group B.
3. Therefore, everyone in group B has quality X.

The second premise—the assumption that individual or subgroup "A" is a perfect representative of the entire population of group "B"—is both the defining feature of stereotypes and their greatest weakness. For that reason, a speaker who does not wish to draw attention to the fact that his or her argument is based on a stereotype might deliver the argument as a simple assertion, such as, "Left-handed people are liars."

When debunking an argument that is based on a stereotype, remember to attack the weakest premise of the argument—the idea that "A" (e.g., a politician, a group of left-handed people, etc.) is a perfect representative of an entire group of people. As with other hasty generalizations, and weak analogies in general, the downfall of the stereotyping fallacy is the fact that it assumes sameness and overlooks significant differences. They form assumptions about an entire population based on an individual member of the group, creating an analogy between a part and the whole.

Exercise 1: Identification

Each of the following arguments uses a common saying to support its conclusion. Some of the arguments are examples of strong analogies, some are weak analogies, and some do not contain analogies at all.

Identify each of the following as a strong analogy ("strong"), a weak analogy ("weak"), or another form of expression ("other"). Explain your answer.

1. Pride goes before a fall, so you should stop bragging so much.

2. A chain is only as strong as its weakest link, so we should remove the worst players from our team.

3. A rolling stone gathers no moss, so it's best to stay in one place.

4. God looks after drunks and fools, so I'm sure he will look after you.

5. A leopard cannot change its spots, so I wouldn't expect Peter to stop lying.

Exercise 2: Explanation

Each of the following passages contains an analogy. Explain which objects are being compared in the analogy and what conclusion is drawn. Then, rephrase the analogy in the following format:

    1. A is like B.
    2. A has property X.
    3. B also has property X.

1. "Govern a great nation as you would cook a small fish. Do not overdo it." —Lao Tsu

2. "[A] great Empire, like a great cake, is most easily diminished at the edges." –Benjamin Franklin (from the essay, "Rules By Which A Great Empire May Be Reduced To A Small One")[14]

---

[14] *The Public Advertiser*, September 11, 1773

Exercise 3: Imitation

Create an example of a legitimate analogy and an example of a weak analogy. Then, for each analogy, translate your argument into the following format:

1. *Premise.*
2. *Premise.*
3. *Conclusion.*

Finally, explain the difference between the legitimate analogy and the fallacious analogy.

Exercise 4: Evaluation

The following passage comes from Fyodor Dostoyevsky's The Brothers Karamazov. *Read the segment carefully. Then, complete the following steps.*

"But to return to the eldest son," Ippolit Kirillovitch went on. "He is the prisoner before us. We have his life and his actions, too, before us; the fatal day has come and all has been brought to the surface. While his brothers seem to stand for 'Europeanism' and 'the principles of the people,' he seems to represent Russia as she is. Oh, not all Russia, not all! God preserve us, if it were! Yet, here we have her, our mother Russia, the very scent and sound of her. Oh, he is spontaneous, he is a marvelous mingling of good and evil, he is a lover of culture and Schiller, yet he brawls in taverns and plucks out the beards of his boon companions. Oh, he, too, can be good and noble, but only when all goes well with him. What is more, he can be carried off his feet, positively carried off his feet by noble ideals, but only if they come of themselves, if they fall from heaven for him, if they need not be paid for. He dislikes paying for anything, but is very fond of receiving, and that's so with him in everything. Oh, give him every possible good in life (he couldn't be content with less), and put no obstacle in his way, and he will show that he, too, can be noble. He is not greedy, no, but he must have money, a great deal of money, and you will see how generously, with what scorn of filthy lucre, he will fling it all away in the reckless dissipation of one night. But if he has not money, he will show what he is ready to do to get it when he is in great need of it. But all this later, let us take events in their chronological order."

1. Identify what group of people is described in this passage.

2. Briefly describe how the group is characterized.

3. Determine whether the description constitutes an example of stereotyping, explaining your conclusion and providing support from the passage.

Loaded Question:

There's no right answer to a loaded question.

Each of the fallacies we've discussed so far has been a fallacy of argumentation. The **loaded question**, however, is a **fallacy of interrogation**. Rather than being a flawed argument, this type of fallacy occurs in the form of a question.

Loaded questions are laden with assumptions. They are designed to be impossible to answer without making a concession of some kind. The question, "Have you stopped beating your wife yet?" is a perfect example of this underhanded tactic.

The purpose of this technique is to trick an opponent into conceding one or more points that have not been agreed upon or proven. Rather than setting forth premises one by one and attempting to prove them, the individual who commits this kind of fallacy speaks as if the premises are obviously true and need not be proven or even discussed. For example, the question "Have you stopped beating your wife yet?" implies that the person in question has at some point beaten his wife. Because the question is framed to require a response of either "yes" or "no," the respondent appears to have only two possible options for answering the question:

a. "Yes; I have stopped beating my wife."
b. "No; I still beat my wife."

However, there is a third option that may not be apparent at first. If neither of the options is suitable, the best possible response to this kind of question is to point out that the question is fallacious and then suggest an "option c" that more accurately reflects the truth. For instance, in this case, an appropriate response may be,

c. "I have never beaten my wife."

Using the example, "Have you stopped beating your wife yet," we can see that loaded questions often combine two questions. This particular question can be broken down into "Have you ever beaten your wife?" and, if the response is affirmative, "Have you stopped beating your wife?"

In the following example, which is taken from Voltaire's *Candide*, the speaker combines quite a number of assumptions into a single "yes or no" question.

> *"Do you think," said Candide, "that men have always massacred each other, as they do today? Have they always been liars, cheats, traitors, brigands, weak, flighty, cowardly, envious, gluttonous, drunken, grasping and vicious, bloody, backbiting, debauched, fanatical, hypocritical, and silly?"*[15]

---

[15] This question is posed by the title character, Candide, in Chapter 21 of Voltaire's *Candide*. (Voltaire is the pen name of French philosopher and writer François-Marie Arouet.)

In this case, despite the numerous unproven premises that are built into the question, the respondent still appears to have only two responses to choose from:

a. "Yes—people are, and always have been, liars, cheats, traitors, brigands, weak, flighty, cowardly, envious, gluttonous, drunken, grasping and vicious, bloody, backbiting, debauched, fanatical, hypocritical, and silly, as they are today."

b. "No—people have not always been liars, cheats, traitors, brigands, weak, flighty, cowardly, envious, gluttonous, drunken, grasping and vicious, bloody, backbiting, debauched, fanatical, hypocritical, and silly, as they are today."

Whether answering "yes" or "no," the respondent must concede that people are currently liars, cheats, traitors, etc. Thus, the entire, detailed characterization of humanity is treated as a premise that need not be proven. The only question is whether people have *always* matched this description. A more honest approach would be to deal with each issue separately. First, the speaker must deal with the issue of whether humans are currently liars, then cheats, then traitors, and so on until he has included each characteristic. The question of whether this has always been the case becomes relevant only after the respondent has assented to each individual premise.

If the respondent does not agree with the questioner's characterization of humanity, he or she should point out that the question is loaded with assumptions and proceed to explain his or her true stance on the subject (e.g., "People are cheats and liars, but not traitors or cowards; they have not always been this way").

Loaded questions can come in many forms. Here are just a few examples of what a loaded question might look like:

"Who do you think will win the election: the lying con artist or the cheating hypocrite?"
"What do you think of the corrupt two-party system?"
"Where does Santa Claus really live?"
"When did you stop trying to get to work on time?"
"Why do gun owners like violence so much?"
"How can we ensure that rabid squirrels are no longer a threat to the lives of our citizens?"

In each of these cases, the questioner is attempting to force his or her opinion on the respondent.

It's important to keep in mind that there are situations in which it is in fact appropriate to ask a compound question. These include:

1. Asking about an issue that has already been resolved in the discussion (e.g., asking "Have you *always* been a thief?" of someone who has already admitted to being a thief).

2. Asking a rhetorical question—a thought-provoking question that requires no response (e.g., "Here was Caesar! When comes such another?").

3. Asking about a fact that's considered common knowledge or an experience that is considered universal (e.g., "Why is the sky blue?" or "When did you get your first driver's license?")

The term "loaded question" is frequently misused. People often call a question "loaded" simply because it is difficult to answer. Perhaps even more often, people use the term when they are asked about an emotionally charged subject. This mistake may be due, in part, to confusion about the difference between "loaded questions" and "loaded language." The expression "loaded language" actually describes a biased or emotionally manipulative choice of words. Calling cigarettes "cancer sticks" is an instance of loaded language. Of course, the two techniques can also be combined. For example, "Will you do your part to stop the murder of thousands of innocent chickens?" is a loaded question that uses loaded language.

Outside of these circumstances, asking more than one question in a single sentence is a fallacious method of questioning.

So, have you stopped asking loaded questions yet?

Exercise 1: Identification

For each of the following, determine whether the question is legitimate or "loaded." Explain your answer.

1. How long has France been an evil country?

2. Has grass always been green?

3. Is it still immoral to sell cigarettes now that everyone knows they cause cancer?

4. When will there be justice in Tibet?

5. Do you know when Alaska became a state?

Exercise 2: Explanation

Each of the following quotes contains a question that contains one or more assumptions. For each, identify the assumption(s) contained in the question.

1. "How many times must the cannon balls fly / before they're forever banned?" —Bob Dylan, "Blowin' in the Wind"

2. "How much longer are we going to think it necessary to be 'American' before (or in contradistinction to) being cultivated, being enlightened, being humane, and having the same intellectual discipline as other civilized countries?" —Edith Wharton

3. "Our study was set up to explore why some people can exercise self-control, while others simply cannot." —a professor of psychology

Exercise 3: Imitation

Create an example of a loaded question. Then, describe the assumption(s) that are inherent in the question. Finally, break the question into two or more distinct questions, dealing with one issue at a time.

Example:

"What can we do to stop the spread of Marxist propaganda in our schools?"

This question assumes both that Marxist propaganda is currently being spread in schools and that this propaganda must be stopped. The question could be broken down into the following questions: "Is Marxist propaganda being spread in schools? If so, should we try to stop the spread of this propaganda?"

Exercise 4: Evaluation

The following passage is an excerpt from the gospel account of John.[16] *In this dialogue, we see an example of a loaded question and a model of an appropriate response to this kind of fallacy. Read the passage carefully, and then complete the following steps:*

1. Explain what assumption is contained within the loaded question.

2. Rewrite the question in a way that eliminates the unwarranted assumption contained in the original question.

3. In your own words, explain the response to the question that appears in the passage.

> "As [Jesus] passed along, He noticed a man blind from his birth. His disciples asked Him, 'Rabbi, who sinned, this man or his parents, that he should be born blind?'
>
> Jesus answered, 'It was not that this man or his parents sinned, but he was born blind in order that the workings of God should be manifested (displayed and illustrated) in him.'"

---

[16] John 9:1-3 (AMP)

Red Herring:

Throwing the hounds off the scent

A **red herring** argument diverts attention from the true issues of a debate by emphasizing irrelevant information.[17]

The idiomatic use of the term "red herring" has its origins in the practice of using fish to train hunting dogs. At one time, it was common practice for English fox hunters to use the reddish-colored flesh of smoked herring to create false trails for their hounds to follow, thus training the dogs to follow a scent. Through this association, the term "red herring" has become a shorthand metaphor for any diversionary tactic that essentially creates a "false trail."

The red herring fallacy is often used to divert attention from a weakly presented or ill-founded argument. The following dialogue from Fyodor Dostoevsky's *The Brothers Karamazov* contains a humorous example of the use of the red herring technique in a poorly reasoned argument. In the bolded passage, we see an illustration of how the red herring fallacy often appears in casual conversation. In this instance, the speaker, Fyodor Karamazov, attempts to cast doubt on the concept of Hell by arguing that it can exist only if it has a ceiling and if its demons are equipped with hooks. Lacking a logical defense for his skepticism over the concept of Hell, he grasps for a defense through these inconsequential details.

> *So you want to be a monk? . . . . You'll pray for us sinners; we have sinned too much here. I've always been thinking who would pray for me, and whether there's anyone in the world to do it . . . . It's impossible, I think, for the devils to forget to drag me down to hell with their hooks when I die. Then I wonder—hooks? Where would they get them? What of? Iron hooks? Where do they forge them? Have they a foundry there of some sort? The monks in the monastery probably believe that there's a ceiling in hell, for instance. Now I'm ready to believe in hell, but without a ceiling. It makes it more refined, more enlightened, more Lutheran that is. And, after all, what does it matter whether it has a ceiling or hasn't? But, do you know, there's a damnable question involved in it?* **If there's no ceiling there can be no hooks, and if there are no hooks it all breaks down, which is unlikely again, for then there would be none to drag me down to hell, and if they don't drag me down what justice is there in the world?** *Il faudrait les inventer,*[18] *those hooks, on purpose for me alone, for, if you only knew, Alyosha, what a blackguard I am.*

---

[17] In addition to being the name of a logical fallacy, the term "red herring" also describes a device often used in suspense literature, such as mystery novels. In the literary context, a "red herring" is usually a misleading set of clues the author includes to keep readers from guessing a surprise ending, such as the revelation of the murderer's identity at the end of the novel.

[18] "It would be necessary to invent them."

When used well, the red herring technique can be highly effective at sidetracking audiences. Nevertheless, it's inadvisable to use any form of red herring because doing so can damage a speaker's ethos, making him or her seem desperate and dishonest. Committing this fallacy can also ruin a good argument by making it seem too weak to stand on its own.

There are many varieties of red herring fallacies, and each sub-type in this category describes a particular approach to distraction. In the pages that follow, we'll discuss a few of the most common types of red herring fallacies.

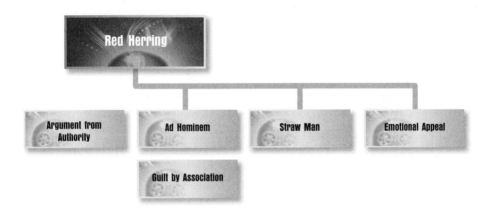

Argument from Authority:
Four out of five experts recommend it.

An **argument from authority** is one that places undue emphasis on the opinion of the speaker or another presumed expert.

Not all arguments that cite the opinion of an expert are fallacious; in fact, in many situations, listening to the opinion of someone who has a great deal of knowledge and experience with a given topic is the most logical thing to do. We generally give great weight to the opinions of experts when dealing with complex subjects that the average untrained person may have trouble understanding. For instance, it's perfectly reasonable to consider a doctor's opinion about the human body or a mechanic's opinion about an engine.

It's also important to note that all arguments appeal to an ultimate authority of some kind. For instance, modern scientists usually appeal to the evidence in nature that they are able to directly observe or measure as their ultimate authority. The fact that a speaker is appealing to an authority of some kind does not, in and of itself, make an argument weak.

> *Aliases Include:*
>
> • Argument from Misleading Authority
>
> • Appeal to Authority
>
> • Argumentum ad Verecundiam ("argument from respect")

The problem arises when a speaker gives great weight to the opinion of an "expert" who is not really an authority on the subject at hand, or when the speaker treats the opinion of a legitimate expert on the subject as if it were infallible proof. The following examples illustrate these two kinds of arguments from authority.

Citing an inappropriate "expert":
The US Surgeon General uses a PC.
Therefore, PCs are better than Macs.

Citing an expert's opinion as infallible proof:
The US Surgeon General says that no one should ever be allowed to eat trans-saturated fats.
Therefore, no one should ever be allowed to eat trans-saturated fats.

Keep in mind that a speaker can also commit either of these arguments from authority by citing his or her own opinion as infallible or by inappropriately assuming the role of expert. In a legitimate appeal to ethos (a rhetorical technique discussed in the beginning of the book), a speaker attempts to appear credible, using his or her own character and experience to add weight to an argument. By contrast, in a fallacious argument from authority, the speaker uses his or her opinion—or that of another reputed "expert"—to replace or override logic.

There is nothing wrong with using an expert opinion to bolster an argument, if the authority can honestly claim special knowledge of the topic. It's important to remember, however, that in a rational debate, no mere opinion, however well informed, can constitute a sufficient argument in and of itself—at best, an opinion can add credibility to an argument that is well supported by facts.

> *"Anyone who conducts an argument by appealing to authority is not using his intelligence; he is just using his memory."* –LEONARDO DA VINCI

Ad Hominem:
An argument "against the man"

Like other red herring fallacies, **ad hominem** arguments are meant to divert attention from the legitimate issues of the debate. In this particular kind of red herring, the distraction that's offered is an argument "against the man," as a literal translation of the fallacy's Latin name suggests. The speaker who commits this fallacy suggests that an opponent's argument should be rejected on the basis of some quality of the speaker that is not logically related to the credibility of his or her argument. In effect, this approach deflects attention from an opponent's argument, rather than addressing the argument itself. The following dialogue illustrates what this technique might look like in a debate.

> *"When you have no basis for an argument, abuse the plaintiff."* –CICERO

A: My research demonstrates that using pesticides in the home increases the risk of cancer.

B: Have you had cancer?

A: No.

B: Then you're in no position to know whether pesticides cause cancer.

In this example, speaker B makes an obvious attempt to distract the audience from his opponent's points. Instead of addressing the research his opponent has presented, speaker B attempts to put speaker A's authority in doubt. B claims that A cannot be in a position to make a statistical scientific analysis because he has never experienced cancer. In this case, the attempt falls flat because B's ad hominem attack clearly has no bearing on A's argument. By contrast, a legitimate response to speaker A's presentation would have been focused on the research and the argument presented, rather than on speaker A's personal experience—unless personal experience is a central part of speaker A's argument.

This may not be a realistic argument, but the basic formula it follows is not uncommon in debates we see all the time. Unfortunately, when the issues in question are emotionally charged, it is often more difficult to discern the faulty thought patterns behind these kinds of attacks.

Ad hominem is one of the most common and best-known fallacies. However, many of the statements that are described as ad hominem attacks do not actually commit this logical fallacy. The best way to gauge the legitimacy of a possible ad hominem argument is to determine whether the allegation is designed merely to distract from the issue at hand. If the argument casts legitimate doubts on an opponent's knowledge or personal credibility, the speaker may be making a useful point. Consider the following sensible approach to questioning an opponent's expertise:

A: My research demonstrates that using pesticides in the home increases the risk of cancer.

B: Do you have a degree in medicine or biology?

A: No; I'm a sociologist.

B: Can you tell us more about how you conducted your research?

This approach is not fallacious. In a debate on this topic, it might be perfectly legitimate for a speaker to point out an opponent's relative lack of knowledge of biology or medicine. It would not, however, be appropriate to suggest that an opponent cannot be qualified to enter the debate simply because he has not had personal experience with pesticides or cancer.

As a general rule, it's reasonable to point out an opponent's personal traits if they relate to his or her credibility. In a political debate or murder trial, for example, questioning the individual's character is often acceptable. The further the accusations stray from the facts of the argument, however, the weaker (i.e., more fallacious) an ad hominem appeal becomes.

The best way to defuse an ad hominem argument is to identify it as a mere distraction from the true questions at hand—to point out that the accusation, even if true, does not change the nature of the facts in dispute.

There are several subtypes of the ad hominem fallacy. What follows is just one of several forms this fallacy can take.

Guilt by Association: *Be careful of the company you keep.*

Guilt by association is a type of ad hominem fallacy in which a speaker attempts to malign an opponent by associating him or her with a negative concept. Rather than focusing on the issue at hand, the speaker attempts to fasten the audience's attention on an unpleasant person, idea, or object. The fallacy is based on the false notion that if an individual can be linked in any way to something offensive, it is fair to equate the individual with the offensive object.

One real-life example of this kind of argument can be seen in a political advertisement that was created for Lyndon B. Johnson's 1964 presidential campaign. The commercial, which was never televised because of its controversial approach, attempted to vilify Johnson's opponent, Barry Goldwater, by associating him with the Ku Klux Klan (KKK). The commercial depicted activities and symbols associated with the KKK, accompanied by the following narration:

> 'We represent the majority of the people in Alabama who hate niggerism, Catholicism, Judaism, and all the -isms in the whole world.' So said Robert Creel, Grand Dragon of the Alabama Ku Klux Klan. He also said, 'I like Barry Goldwater, I believe what he believes in.'

In this quote, we see a blatant use of the guilt by association fallacy. Johnson's campaign attempts to malign Goldwater based solely on the fact that he was admired by a leader of the KKK. Without saying it directly, the ad implies that Goldwater represents the same worldview and interests as Robert Creel. The problem is that from the information in this ad, it is impossible to know whether the two men actually agree on substantive issues; all we know is that Creel has endorsed Goldwater. Without any further illustration of bigotry on the part of Goldwater himself, this argument would be fallacious even if Goldwater were actually as bigoted as Creel. In reality, Goldwater had rejected Creel's endorsement before the advertisement was made.

Straw Man:
Sparring with a scarecrow

Like each of the other red herrings we've discussed, **straw man** arguments are a diversionary tactic. In this particular fallacy, the speaker avoids addressing an opponent's argument directly by creating and attacking a "dummy" argument that does not accurately represent the opponent's stance. That is, rather than addressing the opponent's real argument, the speaker describes a different argument—usually one that is rather outlandish and easy to dismantle. It's as if the speaker is attacking a mere scarecrow—a limp, lifeless caricature of the opponent's true stance.

A straw man argument need not be a spectacular departure from an opponent's real argument; sometimes a speaker will mischaracterize his or her opponent's stance in a subtle way, altering a few key details. Most straw man arguments will exaggerate the opposition's stance to some degree, making it seem more extreme than it actually is.

For an example of a straw man argument, we can look to Voltaire's *Candide*. In this satirical novella, Voltaire mocks the ideas of his contemporary, philosopher Gottfried Leibniz. Using the character of Professor Pangloss to voice a distorted version of Leibniz's arguments, Voltaire misrepresents Leibniz's philosophy as blind, misguided optimism, rather than acknowledging the complexity of Leibniz's views. Among other absurd-sounding remarks, Pangloss insists repeatedly that "All is for the best in this best of all possible worlds," despite the fact that he is surrounded by disaster and tragedy. Thus, in the character of Pangloss, Voltaire creates a "straw man" that can be ridiculed easily, rather than confronting Leibniz's actual arguments and taking into account their complexity and nuances.

While Voltaire presented his straw man argument in literary form, the fallacy can be found in any kind of situation that involves a debate on viewpoints. For an example of what this fallacy often looks like, consider the following argument you might hear in a discussion of politics:

> *The Senator from Vermont has suggested that we dismantle our North Atlantic Radar system, now that the Soviet Union is no longer a threat. I don't understand why he would want the United States to be defenseless.*

In this argument, the speaker exaggerates the Senator's viewpoint, saying that he "want[s] the United States to be defenseless," making this a straw man argument. Whenever a speaker describes an opponent's argument in a dishonest way, instead choosing to represent a distorted, extremist, or simply absurd version of the argument that can easily be dismissed, he or she is committing the straw man fallacy. The best way to dismantle this kind of argument is to point directly to the differences between the actual argument one is presenting and the distorted or oversimplified version of the argument the opponent has created.

Emotional Appeal:
Listen to your heart.

An ***emotional appeal*** is a red herring fallacy in which a speaker attempts to persuade an audience through emotional manipulation. Like all forms of the red herring fallacy, appeals to emotion offer a distraction from the true issues in question. In this case, the distraction presented is one that arouses strong feelings. The speaker relies heavily on a pathetic appeal, to the neglect of logic.

Aliases Include:

• **Argument from Emotion**

Sub-Fallacies Include:

• **Appeal to Anger**

• **Appeal to Fear**

• **Appeal to Pity**

• **Appeal to Ridicule**

Example:

You should eat everything on your plate because there are starving children in Africa.

This argument can be rewritten as follows:

1. There are starving children in Africa. Premise
2. Therefore, you should be grateful that you have food. Inferred premise
3. Therefore, you should eat everything on your plate. Conclusion

However compelling this argument might seem, it is a weak argument from a logical standpoint; the truth of its premises does not strongly suggest the truth of its conclusion. While the image of starving children may rightly inspire gratitude, it does not provide a rationale for eating whatever food happens to be on one's plate. In fact, rather than providing a logical reason for a certain way of behaving or thinking, this argument attempts to persuade through an appeal to guilt.

Fallacious appeals to emotion cover the entire range of human feelings. They often evoke negative feelings, like envy (*argumentum ad invidiam*) and fear (*argumentum ad metum*). However, benevolent emotions, like pity (*argumentum ad misericordiam*), can also be abused using this same fallacious tactic.

In the beginning of this book, we discussed the legitimate persuasive use of rhetorical appeals to pathos—and, indeed, appealing to an audience's emotions is a perfectly reasonable and justifiable approach in some cases. Specifically, pathos is best used in arguments that attempt to persuade one to take a particular course of action based on a predictable direct outcome. For instance, appealing to fear when convincing a child not to play with matches is a legitimate use of pathos in persuasive communication.

Example:

Don't play with matches; you could set the house on fire.

Likewise, if a speaker is appealing for charity, it's reasonable to appeal to the audience's pity.

Example:

If you don't donate your kidney, your uncle is not likely to survive much longer.

Notice that in these examples, there is a direct link between the outcome described (e.g., donating a kidney to one's uncle) and the action recommended (e.g., saving the uncle's life). In any legitimate emotional appeal, there is a logical connection between the action and the emotionally charged outcome, and the emotional appeal is not used to override or take the place of reason.

Example:

The engineers made a few miscalculations in designing the space shuttle, but they put a lot of effort into it. They'd be disappointed if we asked them to start over.

In this instance, the speaker is suggesting that a decision be made purely on the basis of emotion, while leaving out the practical (and emotional) implications of using a faulty design—which could include enormous financial expenses and possibly a loss of human lives. The best approach to rebutting an emotional argument is to clearly define where emotion is at play in the argument and where logic and emotion diverge. In the case of the space shuttle, for instance, it might be helpful to point out that the feelings of the engineers have nothing to do with whether the shuttle will launch properly.

Exercise 1: Identification

Each of the following statements exemplifies a type of red herring fallacy from the previous chapter. Identify which type of fallacy most accurately describes each statement.

1. Senator Fink would like us to wage war against any country that fails to obey our every wish.

2. He doesn't seem to value the many thousands of lives that will be lost—or the tears of the thousands of mothers who will have to hear that their sons are never coming home again.

3. Benjamin Franklin once said, "There never was a good war or a bad peace."[19] If one of our founding fathers believed that war was always a bad thing, I think we, too, should agree that this war is a bad idea.

4. Would you rather listen to Benjamin Franklin or to Senator Fink, who failed a history class in college?

---

[19] From a letter to Josiah Quincy (September 11, 1783)

Exercise 2: Explanation

Each of the following arguments appeals to the emotions. For each, identify whether the argument represents a legitimate appeal to pathos or a fallacious emotional appeal.

1. Americans spend an estimated twenty billion dollars annually on ice cream. That amount of money could feed eighty-three million hungry children for an entire year. The whole world would be better off if Americans would stop eating ice cream.

2. Americans spend an estimated twenty billion dollars annually on ice cream. That amount of money could feed eighty-three million hungry children for an entire year. Americans are selfish.

3. Americans spend an estimated twenty billion dollars annually on ice cream. That amount of money could feed eighty-three million hungry children for an entire year. Americans could easily help alleviate hunger in other parts of the world by sending a few dollars a month that they might have otherwise spent on something like ice cream to the World Hunger Campaign.

Exercise 3: Imitation

Create an example of a legitimate argument that appeals to an authoritative source. Then, create an example of a fallacious argument from authority. Explain what makes one argument strong and the other fallacious.

Example of a strong argument:
1. I have studied plant biology for forty years, and I have never heard of a plant that does not need any light at all to survive.
2. Therefore, there probably aren't any plants that can flourish in total darkness.

Example of a fallacious argument from authority:
1. Thomas Jefferson thought that alliances between nations could be harmful.
2. Therefore, the United States should have no part in the North Atlantic Treaty Organization (NATO).

Exercise 4: Evaluation

The following is an excerpt from Kenneth B. Clark's 1963 interview of Malcolm X.[20] *In this section of the interview, Malcolm X argues against Martin Luther King, Jr.'s policy of non-violent activism. Read the passage carefully. Then, describe each of the two bolded passages as either a legitimate argument or an example of one of the specific kinds of red herring arguments described in the previous chapter. Explain your answer, including why Malcolm X's response does or does not qualify as fallacious.*

Clark: . . . Reverend Martin Luther King preaches a doctrine of non-violent insistence upon the rights of the American Negro. What is your attitude toward this philosophy?

Malcolm X: The white man pays Reverend Martin Luther King, subsidizes Reverend Martin Luther King, so that Reverend Martin Luther King can continue to teach the Negroes to be defenseless. **That's what you mean by non-violent: be defenseless. Be defenseless in the face of one of the most cruel beasts that has ever taken a people into captivity.** That's this [sic] American white man. And they have proved it throughout the country by the police dogs and the police clubs. . . . **And just as Uncle Tom, back during slavery, used to keep the Negroes from resisting the bloodhound, or resisting the Ku Klux Klan, by teaching them to love their enemy, or pray for those who use them spitefully, today Martin Luther King is just a 20ᵗʰ century or modern Uncle Tom, or a religious Uncle Tom, who is doing the same thing today, to keep Negroes defenseless in the face of an attack, that Uncle Tom did on the plantation to keep *those* Negroes defenseless in the face of the attacks of the Klan in that day**.

---

[20] The full text of this interview can be found in *The Negro Protest: James Baldwin, Malcolm X, Martin Luther King Talk with Kenneth B. Clark* (1963).

Glossary of Terms

abductive reasoning: a precursor to deductive and inductive thought; the process of developing a hypothesis or a "hunch" based on a limited amount of information

ad hominem: a kind of red herring fallacy; suggests that an argument should be rejected on the basis of some irrelevant quality of the speaker

ambiguous: having more than one possible meaning or interpretation

analogy: compares two or more unlike objects on the basis of a shared quality

    argument by analogy: claims that since two items have a given attribute in common, they must also share a second, distinct point of similarity; an argument of the form:
      1. A is like B.
      2. B has property X.
      3. Therefore, A also has property X.

    weak analogy: fallacy in which the differences between the objects of comparison in an analogy are so significant that they actually defeat the argument, and the comparison between the two items does not lead to the conclusion given

appeal to ethos / ethical appeal: see "ethos"

appeal to logos / logical appeal: see "logos"

appeal to pathos / pathetic appeal: see "pathos"

argument: in logic, a set of connected statements (known as "premises") that are meant to prove a particular conclusion

argument by analogy: see "analogy"

argument from authority: an argument that places undue emphasis on the opinion of the speaker or another presumed expert, committed when a speaker gives great weight to the opinion of an "expert" who is not really an authority on the subject at hand, or when the speaker treats the mere *opinion* of an expert as infallible proof

audience: the person or people who receive the message (i.e., the readers, listeners, or observers)

bandwagon effect: the human tendency to make decisions on the basis of the majority opinion

causation: the act of producing an effect (example: "Falling down the stairs caused Jennifer to break her arm.")

classical appeals: see "rhetorical appeals"

clustering illusion: the human tendency to perceive patterns where no pattern exists

cogency: in inductive reasoning, an argument that is strong *and* consists of premises that are all true

cognitive biases: hard-wired preferences for certain flawed reasoning patterns

conclusion: the main idea that an argument is designed to prove; an argument's thesis

confirmation bias: the tendency to view information in a way that validates our existing opinions and beliefs

correlation: the relationship between two factors (example: "The increase in temperature was correlated with a simultaneous increase in gas prices.")

cum hoc, ergo propter hoc: occurs when a speaker assumes there is a causal relationship between two factors simply because they occur at the same time

deductive reasoning: a type of reasoning in which a conclusion is drawn as a logical consequence of the premises—it *must* be true if the premises are true; the conclusion will not add any new information to the argument, instead simply combining the principles stated in the premises

emotional appeal: a type of red herring fallacy in which the speaker elicits strong emotions to distract the audience from the facts of the argument

ethos: moral character

    appeal to ethos / ethical appeal: an attempt to persuade by establishing the strength of the speaker's credibility

fallacy of interrogation: a form of question that is logically flawed

framing bias: occurs when an individual is presented with two identical options that are described in different terms and responds differently depending on how the issue is presented, or "framed"

gambler's fallacy: the mistaken belief that the results of a random event, like a coin toss, will affect the probability of future outcomes

guilt by association: a type of ad hominem fallacy in which a speaker attempts to malign an opponent by associating him or her with a negative concept

halo effect: occurs when an individual is exposed to a person who has one positive quality and automatically attributes other desirable traits to the individual

hasty generalization: a fallacy in which the speaker draws a conclusion based on an unrepresentative sample; a type of weak analogy

illusory superiority: the tendency to erroneously view oneself as superior to others

inductive reasoning: a kind of reasoning in which conclusions reach beyond the scope of the information provided in the premises, speculating about possibilities outside of the facts that the premises establish

inference: the process of drawing a particular conclusion from the available information

loaded question: a multi-part question that requires the respondent to concede a point that has not already been proven or conceded; a fallacy of interrogation

logic: the formal study of reasoning

logical fallacy: an error in reasoning that makes a deductive argument invalid or an inductive argument weak

    informal fallacy: a content-level error that makes an argument weak; informal fallacies usually apply to inductive arguments, but some can apply to deductive arguments as well
    formal fallacy: an error in the structure of an argument that renders a deductive argument invalid

logos: reason, logic, words

    appeal to logos / logical appeal: an attempt to persuade through rational analysis and persuasive language

message: the information the speaker wishes to convey to the audience

modes of persuasion: see "rhetorical appeals"

non causa pro causa: the fallacy of mistaken causation

non sequitur: an umbrella term for all formal (deductive) fallacies

objective: factual; independent of personal opinion or experience

pathos: emotion, especially pity or compassion

> **appeal to pathos / pathetic appeal**: an attempt to persuade by eliciting an emotional response from the audience

persuasion: the act of convincing someone to accept a given opinion or to carry out a particular course of action

post hoc, ergo propter hoc: occurs when a speaker attempts to argue that one thing has caused another simply because one event occurred after the other

premise: a declarative statement that is used to support or prove the point (conclusion) of the argument

red herring: a fallacy in which the speaker diverts attention from the true issues of a debate by emphasizing irrelevant information

rhetoric: the technique or study of communication and persuasion

rhetorical appeals: the three approaches to persuasive rhetoric—ethos, pathos, and logos; also referred to in the text as the "classical appeals" or "modes of persuasion"

self-serving bias: occurs when an individual claims an undue amount of credit for a positive situation or an inadequate amount of blame for a negative condition

soundness: in deductive logic, a valid argument whose premises are all true

speaker: the individual who is delivering the message, whether in writing, speech, or another medium (i.e., the writer, orator, or presenter)

stereotype: a widely accepted, simplistic view of people who belong to a given group; this fallacy is type of hasty generalization, which is itself a sub-type of the weak analogy fallacy.

straw man: occurs when a speaker avoids addressing an opponent's argument directly by instead creating and attacking a "dummy" argument that does not accurately represent the opponent's stance

strength: in inductive reasoning, a measure of the degree to which the premises of an argument suggest its conclusion

subjective: subject to personal opinion; proceeding from an individual's mind or experience

syllogism: a deductive argument composed of two premises (major and minor) and a conclusion

thesis: an idea that a speaker is putting forward for consideration or attempting to prove

truth value: a statement's relationship to the truth; must be either "true" or "false"

validity: in deductive logic, an argument whose premises necessitate its conclusion; an argument in which it is impossible to affirm each of the premises and deny the conclusion without a contradiction

weak analogy: see "analogy"

wishful thinking: forming conclusions based on idealized imagined outcomes, rather than objectively examining the evidence at hand